A DIFFERENT KIND OF CLASSROOM

TEACHING WITH DIMENSIONS OF LEARNING

A Different Kind of Classroom

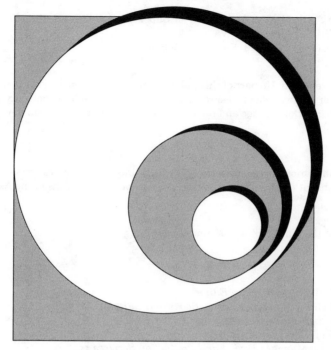

Teaching with
Dimensions of Learning

Robert J. Marzano

**Association for Supervision
and Curriculum Development**

right © 1992 by the Association for Supervision and Curriculum Development,
N. Pitt St., Alexandria, VA 22314.
phone: (703) 549-9110 FAX: (703) 549-3891.

ASCD publications present a variety of viewpoints. The views expressed or implied
in this publication should not be interpreted as official positions of the Association.

Printed in the United States of America.

Ronald S. Brandt, *Executive Editor*
Nancy Modrak, *Managing Editor, Books and Editorial Services*
Julie Houtz, *Senior Associate Editor*
Cole Tucker, *Editorial Assistant*
Gary Bloom, *Manager, Design and Production Services*
Stephanie Kenworthy, *Assistant Manager, Design and Production Services*
Karen Monaco, *Senior Graphic Designer (Cover Designer)*
Keith Demmons, *Graphic Designer*
Valerie Sprague, *Typesetting Specialist*

ASCD Stock No.: 611-92107

Library of Congress Cataloging-in-Publication Data

Marzano, Robert J.
    A different kind of classroom :   teaching with dimensions of
    learning / Robert J. Marzano.
        p.   cm.
    Includes bibliographical references (p.   ).
    ISBN 0-87120-192-5
    1. Teaching.   2. Learning, Psychology of.   3. Curriculum planning—
    United States.   4. Educational tests and measurements—United
    States.   I. Title.
    LB1025.3.M34   1992
    371.1'02—dc20   92-9069
                                                                CIP

❖

A DIFFERENT KIND OF CLASSROOM
TEACHING WITH DIMENSIONS OF LEARNING

❖

❖

Foreword

❖

Reinventing or restructuring America's schools has captured the nation's attention and imagination. Rhetoric abounds with what must now be done to change the way the educational enterprise has been organized, administered, and evaluated.

"Solutions" to improve our nation's schools have ranged from extending the school day or year to creating national standards and assessments. While these *reformations* may in fact enhance educational change initiatives, they do not address "the heart of the matter," and that is the complex systemic and dynamic relationship between how teachers teach and how children learn.

In *A Different Kind of Classroom: Teaching with Dimensions of Learning,* Robert Marzano reviews more than thirty years of research on the learning process and translates it into a model of classroom instruction that he calls Dimensions of Learning. This instructional model is designed to focus our restructuring efforts on authentic student learning by altering the current instructional paradigm to reflect what is now known about how children learn. The Dimensions framework is structured on the premise that the process of learning involves the interaction of five types, or dimensions, of thinking: (1) positive attitudes and perceptions about learning, (2) thinking involved in acquiring and integrating knowledge, (3) thinking involved in extending and refining knowledge, (4) thinking involved in using knowledge meaningfully, and (5) productive habits of mind.

The premise of the five types of thinking emphasizes that learning is a process of constructing meaning. Classroom instruction must systemically promote and develop these dimensions if students are to become constructive learners with enhanced capacity to take increased responsibility for their own learning, and with the knowledge of how to assess their own growth. The ultimate goal is for students to become independent learners who have developed the ability to continue to learn throughout their lives.

The importance of the Dimensions framework for genuine educational restructuring and instructional *renorming* is its emphasis on actually using and integrating what we know about learning in the instructional process. Marzano emphasizes the critical need for every teacher to become an expert on learning and to use that knowledge to align and integrate curriculum, instruction, and assessment to support genuine understanding. Dimensions of Learning provides a basic framework for understanding the teaching-learning dynamic within the classroom and for enhancing the learning partnership between the teacher and the learner.

In our efforts to create learning communities that foster complex creative and ethical thought, Dimensions of Learning refocuses our restructuring initiatives on student learning, which is the foundation of long-lasting success in our classrooms.

—STEPHANIE PACE MARSHALL
ASCD President, 1992–93

❖

Preface

❖

Dimensions of Learning is an instructional program that grew out of the comprehensive research- and theory-based framework on cognition and learning called Dimensions of Thinking (which was the subject of a book of the same name published by the Association for Supervision and Curriculum Development in 1988). Dimensions of Learning translates the research and theory explicated in Dimensions of Thinking into a practical model that K–12 teachers can use to improve the quality of teaching and learning in any content area. More than ninety educators were part of the Dimensions of Learning Research and Development Consortium that worked for two years to shape the basic program into a valuable tool for reorganizing curriculum, instruction, and assessment.

Implicit in the Dimensions of Learning model are six basic assumptions:

1. Instruction must reflect the best of what we know about how learning occurs.

2. Learning involves a complex system of interactive processes that includes five types of thinking—the five dimensions of learning.

3. What we know about learning indicates that instruction focusing on large, interdisciplinary curricular themes is the most effective way to promote learning.

4. The K–12 curriculum should include explicit teaching of higher-level attitudes and perceptions and mental habits that facilitate learning.

5. A comprehensive approach to instruction includes at least two distinct types of instruction: one that is more teacher-directed and another that is more student-directed.

6. Assessment should focus on students' use of knowledge and complex reasoning rather than on their recall of low-level information.

The Dimensions of Learning program includes a variety of components designed to help educators fully understand how these six assumptions affect the teacher's work in the classroom.

A Different Kind of Classroom: Teaching with Dimensions of Learning explores the theory and research underlying the framework. Although teachers need not read this book to use the program, they will have a better understanding of cognition and learning if they do. The *Dimensions of Learning Teacher's Manual* contains detailed descriptions of the instructional strategies inherent to the framework, the decisions the teacher must make to use the framework in the classroom, and the kinds of assessment that support the five dimensions. For each dimension, there are many classroom examples as well as a unit planning guide and assessment forms that teachers can use in their own classrooms. The *Dimensions of Learning Trainer's Manual* contains scripts, overhead transparencies, and guidelines for conducting comprehensive training and staff development in the Dimensions program. *Implementing Dimensions of Learning* explains the different ways the program can be used in a school and discusses the various factors that must be considered when deciding which approach to use. Finally, a set of Dimensions of Learning videotapes introduces and illustrates some of the important concepts underlying the Dimensions model. Together, these resources guide educators through a structured, yet flexible, approach to improving curriculum, instruction, and assessment.

—ROBERT J. MARZANO

1

❖

Learning-Centered Instruction: An Idea Whose Time Has Come

❖

The first wave of reform has broken over the nation's public schools, leaving a residue of incremental changes and an outmoded educational structure still firmly in place. The second wave must produce strategic change that restructures the way our schools are organized and operate. We've been tinkering at the margins of the education problem for too long. It's time now to get to the heart of the matter.

—David Kearns, Deputy Secretary
of Education (1988, p. 565)

I believe that the "heart of the matter" of any educational reform or restructuring is the relationship between the teaching and learning processes. We know that effective teaching mirrors effective learning, yet as educators we have not mounted a serious effort to organize teaching around the learning process. Instead, we have viewed education as an institution or an administrative system or a set of instructional techniques (Banathy 1980). We have not examined the learning process and then built instructional systems, administrative systems, indeed, entire educational systems that support what we know about the learning process. We have not built education from the bottom up, so to speak.

We have not done so because until relatively recently we knew very little about the learning process. As late as 1960, behavioral psychologists viewed the processes underlying cognition and, consequently, the processes underlying learning as existing in a sealed "black box." John Anderson (1990) explains that from its beginnings in 1920, the behaviorist tradition all but eliminated any serious inquiry into the cognitive processes underlying learning. Behaviorism dominated psychology for over forty years. It was not until the advent of cognitive psychology in the 1960s that psychologists began to study the underlying processes in learning. Since then, researchers in cognitive psychology and the related fields of artificial intelligence and cognitive science have created an explosion of knowledge about learning. Over the last three decades, we have amassed enough research and theory about learning to devise a truly learning-based model of instruction.

The ultimate act of restructuring is to change the process of instruction and its related acts (planning, curriculum design, and assessment) so that they reflect the best of what we know about learning. This book is meant as a step in that direction. In it, I attempt to articulate a theory of learning based on the best available research on learning and then translate that theory into a model of classroom instruction that directly affects how teachers plan for instruction, design curriculum, and assess student performance. The model of instruction on which this book is based assumes that the process of learning involves the interaction of five types of thinking, what I call the five Dimensions of Learning. These five dimensions of learning are direct descendants of the Dimensions of Thinking framework (Marzano, Brandt, Hughes, Jones, Presseisen, Rankin, and Suhor 1988). The Dimensions of Thinking model was meant to influence the *theory* of schooling, whereas its progeny is meant to influence the *practice* of schooling. Indeed, some ninety practicing educators from eighteen school districts in the United States and Mexico have contributed to the development of the Dimensions of Learning model.

The five dimensions of learning are loose metaphors for how the mind works during learning. Certainly there are not five independent types of thinking that occur during learning; learning involves a complex system of interactive processes. But metaphors can open our eyes to new ways of seeing, prompting us to explore options that we might not have pursued otherwise. For example, the metaphor that the brain is a computer provides psychologists with powerful insights; so, too, does the metaphor that the brain is a muscle. One metaphor does not negate the other; both are useful. I believe that viewing learning as the product of five dimensions or types of thinking will allow educators to achieve powerful and specific results in the classroom. What are the five dimensions of learning? Let's take a look.

Dimension 1:
Positive Attitudes and Perceptions About Learning

Attitudes and perceptions color our every experience. They are the filter through which all learning occurs. Some attitudes affect learning in a positive way and others make learning very difficult. To illustrate, let's consider the thinking of Jana and Carmen.

Jana's Thinking

Everyone in the 3rd grade seems to be enjoying Mrs. Paynter's demonstration of how the earth revolves around the sun and the moon revolves around the earth. Chad is the sun. He's standing at the front of the class with a flashlight. It's easy for the students to think of Chad as the sun because the flashlight is bright—just like the sun. Sarah is the earth. She's walking around Chad and smiling. Michelle is the moon. She's walking around Sarah as Sarah walks around Chad. Michelle almost has to run to get around Sarah before Sarah gets around Chad. The students enjoy the demonstration, especially the part where Michelle has to run around Sarah. The only one not enjoying the demonstration is Jana. It's not that she doesn't like science; it's her favorite subject. But at recess a few minutes ago, both Sarah and Michelle started teasing her again. You see, Jana has only been in Mrs. Paynter's class for two weeks. She transferred from a school across town and hasn't yet made any friends. In fact, she thinks, Sarah and Michelle seem to be her enemies. They certainly act as though they hate her. They started in on her right from the first day. Jana is so upset that she can't think of much else. She really doesn't learn from Mrs. Paynter's demonstration.

Carmen's Thinking

Carmen isn't looking forward to Mr. Hutchins' science class, even though she thinks Mr. Hutchins' stories are kind of funny, even interesting. It's the way Mr. Hutchins assigns tasks that bothers her. Carmen can't always figure out exactly what she's supposed to do. And Mr. Hutchins usually doesn't give her any help. Last week, for example, Mr. Hutchins gave a great presentation about evaporation and told some interesting stories. When he was done, he asked the class to do Experiment #4 on page 13 of the text. There was only a short paragraph explaining the experiment. Carmen asked Mr. Hutchins to explain the experiment better, but he just told her to read the directions. Ten minutes before class ended, Carmen realized she had done the entire experiment incorrectly. This frustrated her to no end. Now she's worried that the same thing is about to happen again. She can already feel her stomach tightening up in a knot.

These scenarios have at least two elements in common: (1) the teacher was presenting content in an innovative and interesting way, and (2) a student was distracted from effective learning because of specific perceptions. Certainly Mrs. Paynter's demonstration of the solar system and Mr. Hutchins' engaging stories are sound educational practice, but in each of their classes at least one student could not learn effectively because she perceived that something was amiss. Jana felt that she was not accepted by her classmates; Carmen was worried because she was afraid that she wouldn't be able to figure out what Mr. Hutchins expected her to do. The stories of Jana and Carmen both show that attitudes and perceptions affect learning.

One of the major themes in the current research and theory on learning is that attitudes and perceptions play a fundamental role in the learning process. For example, in their review of research in mathematical problem solving, Silver and Marshall (1990) found that learners' perceptions about their ability to solve problems are a primary factor in mathematics performance. If students perceive themselves as poor problem solvers, that perception overrides most other factors, including natural ability and previous learning.

At a more general level, attitudes and perceptions have been described as part of the learner's "self-system," which oversees all other systems (Markus and Ruvulo 1990; Markus and Wurf 1987; McCombs 1986, 1989; McCombs and Marzano 1990). As learners, we continually filter what we are doing through our system of beliefs. Glasser (1981) asserts that learners will even try to change the "outside world" to make it more consistent with the "inside world" of their beliefs. For instance, if you perceive yourself as unacceptable to your peers, you will act in such a way as to make yourself unacceptable. Frank Smith states the case even more strongly:

> What we have in our heads is a theory of what the world is like, a theory that is the basis of all our perceptions and understanding of the world, the soul of all learning, the source of all hopes and fears, motives and expectancies. And this theory is all we have. If we can make sense of the world at all, it is by interpreting our interactions with the light of our theory (Smith 1982, p. 57).

Effective teachers take into account the attitudes and perceptions of the learner and then shape lessons to foster *positive* attitudes and perceptions.

Dimension 2:
Thinking Involved in Acquiring and Integrating Knowledge

Some noneducators think that learning is a process of passively receiving information. More pointedly, they view knowledge as an objective entity that learners must somehow assimilate into their minds. From this perspective, teaching is a process of dispensing information. The teacher moves from student to student, filling each mind with the facts of the lesson. When a well-taught lesson is completed, all students have the same knowledge and understanding of the content.

A radically different perspective of learning has surfaced from the research and theory in cognitive psychology. Cognitive psychologists view learning as a highly interactive process of constructing personal meaning from the information available in a learning situation and then integrating that information with what we already know to create new knowledge. To illustrate, let's consider Miguel's thinking.

Miguel's Thinking

Miguel has really enjoyed this self-defense unit in phys ed because he's been able to learn some kung fu and karate moves. He saw the movie *Karate Kid* four times, so he knows what he'd like to be able to do. Mr. Tully has just demonstrated how to do a "back kick." Miguel thinks this kick looks hard. Although he watched carefully as Mr. Tully went through the steps, he just can't seem to get started. He can't even imagine how to begin. Mr. Tully walks over to him and says, "Miguel, think of the back kick like the side kick—but you do it backwards." He demonstrates once more. All of a sudden, there is a glimmer of understanding in Miguel's eyes. He has a feel for what it might be like to actually do the kick. He gives it a try. His attempted back kick doesn't look like Mr. Tully's, but it's not bad for the first one. Mr. Tully moves on to someone else while Miguel keeps practicing the new kick. With each try, he learns a little more about the back kick. He starts to become aware of things Mr. Tully didn't mention. For example, he discovers that it's a lot easier to keep your balance if you have your feet close together when you start. Also, if you turn your head before you turn your body, you don't get so dizzy when you twirl around. By the end of class, Miguel feels pretty good about this new kick, even though he can't do it very well. He practices the kick every night for the next four days. By the time Mr. Tully's next class rolls around, Miguel can do the back kick as well as he can do any of the other moves he's learned.

Miguel's thinking illustrates a familiar pattern everyone goes through when learning a new skill. Before Miguel could even attempt the kick, he had to relate it to what he already knew how to do. A fundamental principle of learning is that acquiring knowledge involves a subjective process of interaction between what we already know and what we want to learn. We are always using what we know to interpret what we don't know. If we can't link new content to something we already know, learning is much more difficult. For example, read the following paragraph and try to understand it:

> If the balloons popped the sound wouldn't be able to carry since everything would be too far away from the correct floor. A closed window would also prevent the sound from carrying, since most buildings tend to be well insulated. Since the whole operation depends upon a steady flow of electricity, a break in the middle of the wire would also cause problems. Of course, the fellow could shout but the human voice is not loud enough to carry that far. An additional problem is that a string could break on the instrument. Then there could be no accompaniment to the message. It is clear that the best situation would involve less distance. Then there would be fewer potential problems. With face to face contact, the least number of things could go wrong (Bransford and Johnson 1972, p. 719).

Even though you recognize every word in this paragraph, you probably don't understand it. Bransford and Johnson used this passage to demonstrate the power of *schemas*, the name for the way we "package" information in long-term memory. They wrote the passage using a schema that most people have not experienced or would even imagine experiencing, so when you read it you find nothing in your long-term memory that you can use to interact with the information in the passage. If you are given a schema for the passage, however, it is easy to understand. Figure 1.1 on page 8 contains a schema that can be used to interpret the paragraph above. Study it for a moment and then read the passage again. It should be easy to understand this time.

Understanding something, then, depends on our having experiences stored in packets in long-term memory that can interact with the new information presented in a learning situation. Linking our prior knowledge to what we are about to learn is always the first type of thinking we use when acquiring new knowledge. But, as Miguel's story illustrated, learning doesn't stop there. Once we have an initial conception of information, we have to shape it. Miguel had to go through the motions of the back kick many times to discover the finer points of successfully performing it. The importance of this aspect of learning is difficult to overestimate. Our initial understanding of a concept or a process is rarely complete and accurate; we must loop through it several times, trimming it here, expanding it there, finding out what works and what doesn't. If learners do not engage in this personal organizing and shaping process, their understanding will frequently be poor or even inaccurate.

My favorite example of this idea involves my youngest daughter, Ashley. When she was five years old, I made three trips to Cedar Rapids, Iowa, each trip a week after the previous one. During the first two trips, my wife explained to Ashley that I was in a place called Cedar Rapids. Capitalizing on the educational opportunity, my wife described some of the features of Cedar Rapids and even brought out the map to show Ashley exactly where Cedar Rapids is. During the third visit, my wife asked Ashley if she remembered anything about where I was or if she had any questions about where I was. Quite innocently and sincerely, my daughter responded, "Why does Dad keep going back to Peter Rabbit's?" As all learners do, she had used her prior knowledge to interpret this new information. Unfortunately, she had attached to it the wrong background information. It's rather interesting and more than a little humorous to imagine how she was linking her background knowledge of Peter Rabbit to the new information she was given. Of course, my wife corrected the misconception immediately and reviewed the information with her, stressing the correct interpretation, a city in another state.

My daughter's experience resembles most initial learning experiences. Kathleen Roth (1990) provides a wonderful example of how the lack of background knowledge affects children's initial understanding of science concepts. She describes Kevin, a 7th grader who, after learning that plants are like people in that they take in multiple sources of food from the environment, initially concluded the following, which he wrote on a pretest:

> Food (for plants) can be sun, rain, light, bugs, oxygen, soil, and even other dead plants. Also warmth or coldness. All plants need at least three or four of these foods. Plus minerals (Roth 1990, p. 145).

FIGURE 1.1
Schema for Bransford and Johnson Passage

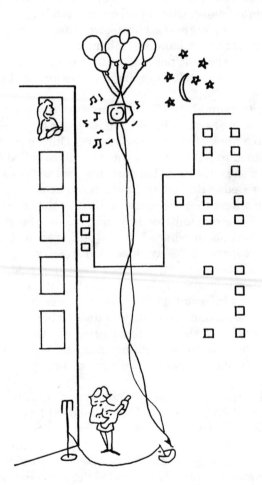

Source: Bransford and Johnson 1972

Obviously, attaching prior knowledge to new information isn't enough. Effective learning requires a more in-depth analysis of the new information to organize and shape it in ways that highlight what's important and to weed out errors.

The final aspect of initially acquiring and integrating knowledge is internalizing information in such a way that it can be readily used. Recall that Miguel had to practice the back kick many times before it became something he could actually use. LaBerge and Samuels (1974) provide a detailed explanation of this aspect of learning. They say that for new information to be useful, it must be learned to such an extent that we do not have to think much about it when we use it. One of the best illustrations of this principle is driving a car. Driving is probably one of the more complex things you do every day: You make split-second decisions. You perform several actions in rapid succession. And you do this at fifty-five miles per hour while having an argument about a football game. You have learned the process of driving a car and the related road rules to such a point that driving has become automatic.

Acquiring and integrating knowledge, then, involves using what you already know to make sense out of new information, working out the kinks in the new information, and assimilating the information so that you can use it with relative ease.

Dimension 3:
Thinking Involved in Extending and Refining Knowledge

Knowledge doesn't remain static, even when we learn it to the point of automaticity. If we continue the learning process, we extend and refine what we know. This dimension of learning, like the others, has some distinguishing characteristics. Let's explore them by considering Joleen's thinking.

Joleen's Thinking

In Ms. Kelter's class, students have just completed reading a chapter about the battle at the Old North Bridge in Concord, which was a beginning point of the Revolutionary War. They have also heard a lecture and watched a film about the historic event. They seem to know it well. They know who participated in the battle, what happened, and even why it happened. At least they know the "why" of the battle as it was described in the lecture and the film. Today Ms. Kelter asks the class to do something different. She divides them into small groups and gives them the following assignment: "Explain how the battle at the Old North Bridge is like something that has happened in the last twenty years."

Joleen, who has an *A* going in the class, asks, "Exactly what are we supposed to compare it with?" Ms. Kelter's answer surprises her. "Anything you want, just show me how they are alike." Almost as a reflex, Joleen responds, "What if we pick the wrong thing?" Again, Ms. Kelter's answer surprises her: "You can't be wrong on this one, as long as you show me how they are alike."

At first, some of the students in Joleen's cooperative group think this is going to be the easiest assignment they have ever had. "We can't be wrong, we can say anything we want." Once they begin, though, they soon change their mind. Joleen says, "What should we pick?" Initially, the members of her group start throwing out wild ideas: "It's like a baseball game." "It's like a wedding." Finally, in frustration Joleen says, "Wait a minute. Stop talking all at once. Let's look at what really happened at the Old North Bridge. Forget about who was there and who did what. What happened in general?" Her classmates look at her with blank stares. She thinks for a while and says, "Here's what I mean: Wasn't it that there was this group of people who expected to be attacked by another bigger group? So this smaller group was just waiting for something to go wrong. Then when they saw some smoke coming from their town they assumed that the British had attacked Concord. I mean, because they were expecting to be attacked, they would probably see the slightest unusual thing as proof that what they expected to happen was actually happening." The other students start to perk up a bit. Mark says, "OK, I see what you're getting at. It's like the riots that happened in L.A. that we studied. Because the people thought the police were going to attack, they saw a really harmless thing as the beginning of the attack."

Joleen and her classmates work on the comparison for the rest of the class period. When they present their comparison the following day, Joleen, who (to no one's surprise) has appointed herself as spokesperson, begins the presentation by saying, "I see the whole thing really differently now; it was all kind of a big mistake."

We can probably safely say that Ms. Kelter's comparison activity changed her students' knowledge of the incident at the Old North Bridge. Joleen's view of the incident certainly changed. Psychologists describe a variety of ways we can change what we "know" even when what we know is accurate. The types of changes they describe range from small changes that occur over time to fairly dramatic changes (Piaget 1954, 1959; Rumelhart and Norman 1981; Vosniadou and Brewer 1987). It is the more dramatic changes that are the focus of Dimension 3, extending and refining knowledge.

Many strategies and activities can help bring about these changes. From my admittedly biased position, I commonly credit the "thinking skills movement" with developing and popularizing many of these techniques. Beyer (1988), de Bono (1985), Swartz (1987), Perkins (1981, 1985), and many others have given us powerful ways of stretching students' knowledge—helping them see things in different ways. As effective as these techniques and strategies are, they still require learners to think at a level that can be a little uncomfortable for them. In keeping, William Chase of Carnegie-Mellon University uses the cliché "no pain, no gain" to describe the energy and effort necessary to develop knowledge to the level associated with expertise (in Anderson 1990, p. 258). In short, teachers and students should never forget that extending and refining knowledge is usually hard work.

Dimension 4:
Thinking Involved in
Using Knowledge Meaningfully

We acquire knowledge or develop a skill so that we can use that knowledge or skill. The type of thinking required to use knowledge is related to the type of thinking necessary to extend and refine knowledge (Dimension 3). It has some unique and important characteristics, though. To illustrate, let's consider Christine's thinking.

Christine's Thinking

The students in Mr. Brandt's class are a little shook up. They've just finished reading a chapter in their textbooks on "climate" that explains how such factors as altitude, humidity, and longitude and latitude affect climate. Before that, they watched a film showing the influence of weather on the environment. Usually they would next be tested on this information and then presented with more information. Today, though, Mr. Brandt isn't going on to the next chapter. Instead, he announces that he wants students to use the information they've just learned. He wants them to "ask some interesting questions you have about the stuff we've just learned." He provides a few examples: "You might want to consider what could happen if the weather patterns changed drastically in our region. Or you might want to use the computer simulation program to test out some of your theories about the different ways weather can be influenced." Mr. Brandt gives the class a choice of five types of projects to work on over the next few weeks. He also tells students they can make up their own projects if they don't like the ones he's dreamed up.

Christine has really enjoyed the unit on weather. One thing that struck her early on is how much money and energy people spend protecting themselves against weather. "We build walls, roofs, heating systems, cooling systems, awnings, and a bunch of other things to keep the weather out. I wonder what a house would be like that tried to *use* weather rather than protect against it." At the end of the class, Christine approaches Mr. Brandt and tells him about her idea for a project. Mr. Brandt is enthusiastic. He provides Christine with some guidance and challenge by saying, "Why don't you see if you can do it within a set budget, using as many different aspects of weather as possible?"

Over the next two weeks, Christine learns more about heating systems, cooling systems, wind-driven turbines, and the like, than she ever thought she wanted to know. Quite frequently, she goes to Mr. Brandt for help. He usually sends her to a book, magazine, or person that has the information she's looking for. Although her final product will simply be a floor plan and a videotaped explanation of the features of her "weather-friendly" house, Christine finds that she has to continually make decisions about what to include and what to exclude in her house. It seems as though any minor change in her plans affects four other things that must also be changed.

When she finishes the project, Christine tells Mr. Brandt that it was the most difficult project she has ever done—and maybe the most rewarding. She now knows why all houses don't use weather more—it's very difficult and very expensive. "But," she adds, "it can be done."

Christine's task was similar to Joleen's (described in Dimension 3) in that both required thinking about content in unusual ways. Both tasks challenged the learners by making them go beyond what they normally do. Christine's task was much more extended than Joleen's, however; Joleen needed to think about and work on her task for a few days, whereas Christine thought about and worked on her task for two weeks. It is the extended engagement in complex tasks that allows for the deepest learning. Theorists such as Norman Frederiksen (1984) have pointed out the inconsistencies between "real-life work" and "school work." In school, students engage in short-term tasks that usually can be completed in one class period. In life outside the school, the tasks we perform take weeks, months, sometimes years to complete. Elliot Jaques (1985) asserts that it is only when we work on long-term projects that the full complement of skills and abilities characteristic of effective learning comes into play.

Christine's task was also heavily self-directed. She was free to select a topic and determine how she would report on it and what resources she would use. Student control is another factor that greatly affects the type and quality of learning. In a series of studies, Susan Harter (1980, 1982) has shown that learners who lack a perceived sense of control will naturally "hold back." Learners need to feel ownership of the task if they are to unleash all their talents and abilities. Providing students with control can be a simple matter of allowing them to choose among alternatives. For example, consider Nancy Atwell's (1987) description of the effects of providing for student choice in the form of sustained silent reading (SSR):

> I began letting my kids read their own books one day each week, and they began driving me crazy. Daily at least one student would ask, "Ms. Atwell, are we having reading today?" I didn't want to hear this. We had reading every day—or at least that was my impression. I felt little pinpricks of conscience whenever someone voiced a desire for more SSR. But there were too many wonderful anthology selections to cover and too many activities to orchestrate . . . (p. 19).

The final characteristic of Christine's task is that it was realistic. Designing a house is the type of task a person might actually undertake. This is exactly the impetus of the "authentic task" movement championed by such theorists as Grant Wiggins (1989). Wiggins and others assert that what is needed in education is a shift from artificial tasks, the purpose of which is to cover content, to more authentic tasks, the purpose of which is to engage learners in complex issues that enhance the learning of content and the ability to learn.

In summary, the fourth dimension of learning, using knowledge meaningfully, demands thinking that is extended over a long period of time, directed by the student, and focused on realistic or authentic issues.

Dimension 5:
Productive Habits of Mind

Our mental habits influence everything we do. Poor habits of mind usually lead to poor learning, regardless of our level of skill or ability. Even skilled learners can be ineffective if they haven't developed powerful habits of mind. To illustrate, let's consider Lorraine's thinking.

Lorraine's Thinking

Lorraine considers herself bright, especially in mathematics. Because her dad is a mathematics professor at the university, she has a lot of help solving her homework problems. In fact, every summer her father has obtained a copy of the math text for the upcoming year and gone over the problems with her. When she has difficulty with a certain type of problem, he has given her hints that make the problem easy. By the time she encounters the problems in school, she already knows exactly what to do. But now she's transferred to a new school and her dad hasn't looked over her new math book. It's the first week of math class. The teacher has just handed out a set of problems. At first, Lorraine is excited. This is a chance to show what she can do. She soon finds out, however, that she's never seen problems like these. She doesn't have any experience to call on. Lorraine tries the first problem but can't figure it out. She moves to the second problem and can't figure out how to solve it either. She begins to panic and stops thinking about the problems altogether. "Dad didn't show me how to do any of these." Soon she gives up, thinking to herself, "These problems are just too hard."

Unfortunately, Lorraine's behavior is not unusual. Many people amass a certain amount of knowledge and skill in a subject, but don't know how to cope when confronted with new situations. I once observed a student teacher who performed well unless her students asked a difficult question. When this happened, she would give up; she would actually stop teaching. Lorraine and the student teacher suffer from the same malady. Their problem is not a lack of skill or ability; it is that they simply give up when answers and solutions aren't readily available. They haven't developed the mental habit of persisting even when answers and solutions are not apparent. They haven't developed the characteristics of true expertise. Researchers and theorists such as Ennis (1987), Paul (1990), Costa (1991), Perkins (1984), Flavell (1976), and Amabile (1983) have identified a number of mental habits that characterize expertise:

- Being sensitive to feedback
- Seeking accuracy and precision
- Persisting even when answers and solutions are not apparent
- Viewing situations in unconventional ways
- Avoiding impulsivity

Operating from these mental habits makes learning effective and efficient. In fact, Lauren Resnick (1987) says that it is operating from these habits that renders thinking higher-order in nature. And for years Arthur Costa (1991) has been extolling the virtues of these "intelligent behaviors." His assertion is that the habits of mind should be at the core of education. What good does it do students to learn content if they do not learn to seek accuracy and precision, avoid impulsivity, work at the edge rather than the center of their competence, and so on? Some educators are rising to Costa's challenge. At least two schools in Denver, Colorado, have patterned their report cards after Costa's habits of mind.

The Relationship Among the Dimensions of Learning

It is important to recognize that the five types of thinking illustrated by the five dimensions of learning do not function in isolation or in a linear order (i.e., first one type of thinking occurs, then another). Instead, they interact in the manner depicted in Figure 1.2 on page 16. All learning occurs within a set of attitudes and perceptions that either promote or inhibit learning (Dimension 1). Learning is also affected by the extent to which a learner uses the productive habits of mind (Dimension 5). Dimensions 1 and 5, then, form the backdrop for learning; thus, they are in the background of Figure 1.2. They are always factors to consider in the learning process.

Given that a learner has attitudes and perceptions conducive to learning and is using effective habits of mind, the learner's first job is to acquire and integrate new knowledge (Dimension 2); that is, the learner must assimilate new knowledge and skills with what she already knows. As we have seen, this is a subjective process of interaction between old and new information. Then, over time, the learner develops new knowledge through activities that help her extend and refine her current knowledge (Dimension 3). The ultimate purpose of learning, though, is to use knowledge in meaningful ways (Dimension 4). As Figure 1.2 indicates, Dimensions 2, 3, and 4 work in concert. As a learner acquires and integrates knowledge (Dimension 2), she also extends and

FIGURE 1.2
How the Dimensions of Learning Interact

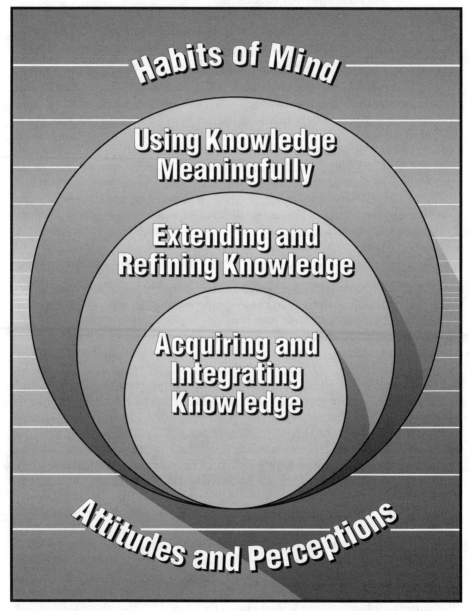

refines it (Dimension 3). And using knowledge meaningfully (Dimension 4) involves extending and refining knowledge.

The five dimensions of learning form a framework that can be used to organize curriculum, instruction, and assessment. In the remainder of this book, I describe in more detail various applications of the Dimensions model. Remember, though, this book is meant to be an introductory companion to the Dimensions of Learning training program. The *Teacher's Manual* for the program (Marzano, Pickering, Arredondo, Blackburn, Brandt, and Moffett 1992) offers multiple strategies described in some depth, whereas this book briefly describes only a few instructional strategies within each dimension, concentrating instead on laying out the research and theory on which the program is based.

2

❖

DIMENSION 1
Positive Attitudes and
Perceptions About Learning

❖

Without positive attitudes and perceptions, students have little chance of learning proficiently, if at all. There are two categories of attitudes and perceptions that affect learning: (1) attitudes and perceptions about the *learning climate* and (2) attitudes and perceptions about *classroom tasks*. A basic premise of the Dimensions of Learning model is that effective teachers continually reinforce attitudes and perceptions in both these categories. The master teacher has internalized techniques and strategies for enhancing these attitudes and perceptions to such a degree that the techniques are frequently transparent: they have become part of the fabric of instruction and are barely noticeable to the undiscerning eye. To illustrate, let's consider Mrs. Salley's class.

Mrs. Salley's Class

It's Monday morning and time for the first-hour class. Mrs. Salley is standing at the doorway, greeting students as they come in. "Hey, Mike, how're you doing?" "Martha, I heard you got a couple of hits in the game last night." When students are seated, Mrs. Salley usually asks them to move into cooperative groups. Today, however, she spends some time going over a few rules and procedures that students seem to be confused about. Although she explained them a week ago, students are ignoring them.

When she questions a few students, she finds that their lack of adherence is more a product of misunderstanding than of disobedience or disregard. She reviews the two rules and asks students what they think about them—if they want to change them in any way. No one seems to really mind the rules. Only a few students ask for some changes. Most of the other students agree that the changes would make the rules better. Mrs. Salley responds, "OK, that sounds reasonable." She writes the new version of the rules on the board and explains that she'll keep them there for a few days just to remind everyone of them. She then asks students to break into cooperative groups. Before they start their assignment, she goes over it in detail, providing students with a model of what things should look like when the task is successfully completed. She says, "This might look a little difficult at first, but you can do it. We've gone over everything you need, so don't get discouraged. I'll help you if you have any problems. Give it your best shot; that's all I'm looking for."

Although this scenario might give the impression that Mrs. Salley was dealing with peripheral issues before she got down to the business of teaching, she was actually setting the stage for learning by attending to specific attitudes and perceptions that affect the learning climate and classroom tasks. Mrs. Salley was dealing with the learning climate when she greeted students at the door, organized them into cooperative groups, and discussed and revised the two classroom rules. And she was attending to attitudes and perceptions about classroom tasks when she provided students with a model of what the successfully completed task might look like. She was also attending to attitudes and perceptions about classroom tasks when she told students that even though the task might look difficult, they had all the skills and abilities necessary to complete it.

The relationship between attitudes, perceptions, and learning is complex. As the above scenario illustrates, however, there are two very general areas on which a teacher can focus with the confidence that her efforts will reap rich rewards.

Fostering Positive Attitudes and Perceptions About the Learning Climate

During the 1980s, the amount of research on the role of classroom climate in the learning process increased tremendously (e.g., Brophy 1982, Fisher and Berliner 1985). Within that body of research and theory, climate was conceptualized in terms of factors external to the learner, such as the quality and quantity of the resources available, the physical environment of the classroom, and so on. More recently, psychologists have begun to view classroom climate more as a function of the attitudes and perceptions of the learner than of elements external to the learner. If students have certain attitudes and perceptions, they have a mental climate conducive to learning. If those attitudes and perceptions are not in place, learners have a mental climate not conducive to learning. In general, two types of attitudes and perceptions affect learners' mental climate: a sense of acceptance and a sense of comfort and order.

Acceptance

Intuitively, we know that learning is inhibited if students do not feel accepted by the teacher and by their peers. You may recall a time in elementary school when you did not feel accepted by your peers, or a time in college when you felt that a professor did not respect you. In both cases, these perceptions probably distracted you more than a little from learning. Researchers confirm the importance of a sense of acceptance. Tom Good and his colleagues (Good 1982, Good and Brophy 1972) have illustrated the importance of students' perceptions of their acceptance by the teacher. Similarly, for decades Arthur Combs (1962, 1982) has championed the importance of students' perceptions of their acceptance.

Virtually all of the research and theory in this area indicate that teachers help students feel accepted in the classroom through seemingly trivial yet very important behaviors. Recall Mrs. Salley's greeting students at the door. This simple act contributes enormously to students' sense of acceptance. In clinical psychology, Robert Carkhuff (1987) has identified specific behaviors that foster acceptance. In education, too, several researchers and theorists have identified and articulated specific techniques to enhance students' perceptions of acceptance. Much of the work of Madeline Hunter (1969, 1976, 1982), for example, and the techniques presented by Kerman, Kimball, and Martin (1980) in the popular Teacher Expectations and Student Achievement (TESA) program deal with activities that enhance students' perceptions of their acceptance. A teacher can foster students' sense of acceptance in many ways:

- By making eye contact with each student in the class, being sure to pay attention to all quadrants of the classroom.
- By calling all students by their first or preferred name.
- By deliberately moving toward and staying close to learners.
- By touching students in appropriate and acceptable ways.

Overtly planning for and using these and related behaviors can help students feel accepted and can also foster teacher insight and awareness. For example, a secondary science teacher once told me that after trying to give eye contact to students in each quadrant of the classroom, she realized that she always avoided looking at students in the left back section of the room. She wondered aloud if she had been doing this all through her fifteen years of teaching and said that if she had, she felt sorry for the hundreds of students who had sat in that part of the room.

Teachers also influence students' sense of acceptance by the manner in which they respond to students' questions. Here are a few basic but powerful behaviors:

• Providing wait time—pausing to allow a student more time to answer instead of moving on to another student when you don't get an immediate response.

• Dignifying responses—giving credit for the correct aspects of an incorrect response.

• Restating the question—asking the question a second time.

• Rephrasing the question—using different words that might increase the probability of a correct response.

• Providing guidance—giving enough hints and clues so that the student will eventually determine the correct answer.

Again, these actions may seem insignificant, but they send powerful messages to students. One teacher told me that she never realized the extent to which she was communicating a lack of acceptance of her students until she began monitoring her responses to their incorrect answers. She found that her usual response was to immediately move on to another student until she received the correct answer. She concluded that her behavior during questioning had highly negative overtones that probably made students reluctant to answer her queries.

Students need to feel accepted by their classmates as well as by their teacher. Although this need has been popularized in recent years through the cooperative learning movement, its importance has been recognized for decades in the research on the social aspects of learning. According to Slavin (1983), research on the utility of cooperative learning was already well developed by the 1920s. From his review of the literature, Slavin has concluded that the positive effects of cooperative learning on academic performance are not well established, but its effectiveness in fostering acceptance and understanding among the members of a group is undeniable.

The most popular model of cooperative learning is probably that developed by Roger and David Johnson (Johnson, Johnson, Roy, and Holubec 1984). In their model, they stress that "individual accountability" and "positive group interdependence" are key elements of cooperative learning. Neither of these dynamics occurs naturally. Teachers have to structure tasks to create individual accountability and group interdependence, usually by asking each group member to be responsible for a different aspect of a task. For example, one member might be responsible for gathering information, another for organizing the information into a cohesive whole, another for orchestrating the best way to report the information, and so on. Individual accountability and positive group interdependence are also fostered by asking students to assume different interaction roles, such as facilitator, recorder, and reporter. It is these very dynamics of cooperative learning that increase the probability of acceptance among group members. Slavin (1984) notes that this probability is heightened when teachers structure cooperative tasks so that groups are mixed in terms of ethnicity, gender, and ability.

Cooperative learning is not the only way to nurture students' sense of acceptance. Based on his theories of psychotherapy, Glasser (1965, 1969) has devised the classroom meeting, a period of thirty to forty-five minutes during which students and teachers set aside their normal academic activities to engage in nonjudgmental discussions of personal, behavioral, or academic problems in an effort to find collective solutions. Glasser describes three types of meetings, each with a slightly different focus. In their discussion of Glasser's model, Joyce and Weil (1986) focus on the social problem-solving meeting, which is usually concerned with behavioral and social problems. It is the group dynamic in such meetings that generates a sense of acceptance among members:

> The orientation of the meeting is always positive—that is, toward a solution rather than toward fault finding. Obviously, many problems do not have a single answer. For example, in the case of coping with a bully, the solution is often in the class discussion itself (Joyce and Weil 1986, p. 207).

Feeling accepted is an important aspect of a positive learning climate. The formal and informal techniques described above can help teachers create this environment.

Comfort and Order

Comfort as described here refers to physical comfort. A student's sense of physical comfort in the classroom is affected by such factors as room temperature, the arrangement of furniture, and the amount of physical activity permitted during the school day. Researchers investigating learning styles have found that students define physical comfort in different ways (Carbo, Dunn, and Dunn 1986; McCarthy 1980, 1990). Some prefer a noise-free room; others prefer music in the air; some prefer a neat, clutter-free space; others feel more comfortable surrounded by their work-in-progress. To accommodate such diversity, many learning-style theorists suggest that students work together to develop group standards for the physical environment of the classroom. For example, as a group, students can decide:

- How to arrange desks and other furniture.
- When to take breaks and what kind of breaks they will be.
- What to display on the bulletin boards and walls.

Presumably, allowing students to make these kinds of decisions keeps in check the teacher's natural tendency to organize the physical environment in a manner that is comfortable for her but not necessarily for her students.

Another important aspect of a sense of comfort is the affective tone of the classroom. Research by Mandler (1983) and others (Santostefano 1986) indicates that a positive affective tone is generally conducive to learning. Most teachers foster a positive affective tone by capitalizing on the lighter side of instruction and even building levity into their daily routine. For instance, I once observed a secondary teacher who had been described to me as "the best of the best," and within five minutes of the start of her class, I found myself laughing. When I reflected on my notes to identify the factors that made her the "best of the best," I concluded that she not only knew the content well and presented it clearly, she also quite consciously got students (and myself) laughing and maintained the jocular tone throughout the lesson. In retrospect, I saw that I had learned a great deal and had fun doing it.

Until recently, little attention has been paid to the importance of positive affect in teaching, but the clinical work of Roger Mills and his colleagues (Mills 1987; Mills, Dunham, and Alpert 1988) has illustrated its central role in learning. Basically, Mills asserts that our affective state at any point in time colors our cognition and behavior. The highest affective state is joy or happiness, and Mills asserts that teachers should overtly attempt to bring about this state whenever possible. Teachers who have for years used humor as a part of their instructional repertoire can take pleasure in knowing that they have been capitalizing on a basic principle of human behavior to enhance student learning.

Order refers to identifiable routines and guidelines for acceptable behavior in the class. Thanks to the research on classroom management

(Anderson, Evertson, and Emmer 1980; Emmer, Evertson, and Anderson 1980), educators have clear directions on how to proceed. For example, we know that explicitly stated and reinforced rules and procedures create a climate conducive to learning. If students don't know the parameters of behavior in a learning situation, the psychological environment can become chaotic. Rules and procedures are commonly established for the following:

- Beginning class
- Ending class
- Interruptions
- Instructional procedures
- Noninstructional procedures
- Grading procedures
- General conduct in the room or school
- Communication procedures

Order also refers to the perception that the learning environment is safe. Although Maslow (1968) established the importance of a sense of safety, it was probably the work of the late Ron Edmonds (1982) that made educators most aware of the importance of a perceived sense of safety in the learning process. At a fairly global level, Edmonds noted that students must believe the school grounds are safe; that is, they must believe they can eat lunch in safety, use the lavatories in safety, walk home in safety, and so on. For the vast majority of American schools, this level of safety has already been secured (although it remains a concern in environments where "gang cultures" have established a foothold).

Students must also believe that they won't be victimized by other students in direct or indirect ways, and that if they are, teachers will immediately intervene. Unfortunately, breaches of safety frequently go unnoticed by teachers. I once interviewed a secondary teacher who was "sure" that students in his homeroom class perceived the school in general and his class in particular as a safe environment. When he asked students to fill out an anonymous questionnaire about their perceptions of safety, however, he discovered that some students in his class were practicing what amounted to extortion—demanding payment for protection.

In summary, teachers need to be aware that their simplest behaviors often determine whether students feel accepted—by both teachers and classmates. And they need to be aware that they can adjust the physical environment of the classroom to make students feel more comfortable.

Fostering Positive Attitudes and Perceptions About Classroom Tasks

Proficient learners believe that the tasks they are asked to perform have value, that they have a fairly clear understanding of what the tasks require, and that they have the resources necessary to complete the tasks. Teachers can use specific classroom techniques to bolster these beliefs.

Task Value

Of the beliefs listed above, the perceived value of tasks is probably the most important to the learner's success. Current research and theory on motivation (McCombs 1984, 1987; Schunk 1990) indicate that learners are most motivated when they believe the tasks they're involved in are relevant to their personal goals. Glasser (1981) and Powers (1973) hypothesize that human beings operate from a hierarchical structure of needs and goals: they must satisfy basic physical needs (e.g., food, shelter) and psychological needs (e.g., acceptance, safety) before being able to form goals—to decide what they are "consciously trying to accomplish" (Schunk 1990). From this perspective, working to develop a positive mental climate, discussed in the previous section, focuses on meeting students' psychological needs. A growing body of research indicates that when students are working on goals they themselves have set, they are more motivated and efficient, and they achieve more than they do when working to meet goals set by the teacher (Hom and Murphy 1985, Schunk 1985). This research strongly implies that if educators expect students to be motivated to succeed at classroom tasks, they must somehow link those tasks to student goals. Some powerful ways of doing this include allowing students to structure tasks around their interests, allowing students to control specific aspects of tasks, and tapping students' natural curiosity.

Overtly gearing tasks to student interests is a simple matter of knowing what students are interested in and then linking tasks to their interests. For example, knowing that many students in her class are fans of professional basketball, a mathematics teacher might use the box scores from the newspaper to illustrate the concept of the "average." Oddly enough, there is little research evidence indicating that teachers are using student interests, except in the area of reading instruction. Morrow (1991) notes that within that body of research, the trend is toward identifying and capitalizing on student interests, especially within literature-based instructional approaches.

Allowing students to specify how tasks will be completed means that assigned tasks are relatively open-ended. For example, an English teacher might review the rules for using commas and then, as a practice activity, ask students to find examples of each rule in whatever kind of material they want to read. A student interested in baseball might use the sports page. A student interested in music might use the written lyrics to popular songs, and so on.

Capitalizing on the natural curiosity of students is another way of making tasks relevant. Human beings are naturally curious. In effect, we are "hard-wired" to want to know why things happen, how they work, what the parts are, what will happen if . . . , and so on (Lindsay and Norman 1977). Teachers can tap this natural curiosity by offering interesting "tidbits" along with content. For example, I once observed a teacher present students with some of the details of Hemingway's life before she asked them to read one of his short stories. Specifically, she described how Hemingway had established a counterintelligence organization called the Crook Factory to deal with the influx of German spies in Cuba and the presence of submarines off its coast during World War II. Students were fascinated by the account and their enthusiasm carried over into their reading of the story.

Task Clarity

Fundamentally, if learners do not have a clear model of how a task will look when it is completed, their efforts to complete the task will often be ineffective. Educators like Hunter (1982) have provided teachers with strong guidelines about how to make tasks and expectations about tasks clear for students. In general, the guidelines suggest that teachers provide models of completed tasks. For example, following the Hunter guidelines, a language arts teacher who has asked students to write an essay might give students an example of a completed essay that illustrates all of the assigned criteria.

Resources

Obviously, students must perceive that they have the necessary materials, time, equipment, and so on, to complete a task. These are external resources. Not so obviously, students must also perceive that they have the necessary internal resources—the "right stuff." Contrary to popular belief, the "right stuff" is not necessarily ability. In fact, current research and theory in psychology indicate that learners commonly attribute success to any one of four causes (Schunk 1990; Weiner 1972, 1983): ability, effort, task difficulty, or luck.

The first two of these, ability and effort, are key elements of motivation. Learners who believe they have the inner resources to successfully complete a task attribute their success to effort; there is no task they consider absolutely beyond their reach. Learners who believe they are good at some things but not so good at others attribute their success to ability; they perceive themselves as incapable of success at some tasks. In the classroom, teachers should continually reinforce the importance of effort and boost students' sense of their ability. Teachers might give powerful examples of how effort paid off in their own lives or in others'. Covington (1983, 1985) suggests that students should occasionally receive rewards (such as grades) based on their efforts rather than on their successful completion of tasks.

Teachers can improve learning by planning ways to improve students' attitudes and perceptions about the classroom climate and about assigned tasks.

Planning to Develop Positive Attitudes and Perceptions About Learning

Good teachers have always tried to foster positive attitudes and perceptions about learning. In a well-run classroom, many of the ways they do so seem to be simply a part of the natural flow of activity. But seemingly transparent behaviors are usually the result of conscious decisions, of teacher planning. Because attitudes and perceptions do play such an important role in learning, teachers must overtly plan and carry out behaviors to ensure that they are reinforced. To explore how a teacher might plan for reinforcing positive attitudes and perceptions, let's consider Ms. Conklin, a junior high school science teacher who has decided to develop a unit on weather. As part of preparing for the unit, she decides to write up a plan for what she will do to reinforce the first dimension of learning.

Ms. Conklin's Planning for Dimension 1

Even though she's been teaching for more than ten years, Ms. Conklin has decided to make sure that she reinforces positive attitudes and perceptions during her unit on weather. She was prompted to review her methods for doing this by a videotape she recently saw of herself in the classroom during her second year as a teacher. What she noticed as she watched the tape was that she used to do some very nice things in her classes that she somehow discarded over the years. For example, she noticed that she would frequently touch students on the shoulder as she walked up and down the aisles, and she remembered that this simple action seemed to create a bond between her and the students, making them feel accepted and cared for. She decides to reinstate some of the old practices that she let lapse.

Ms. Conklin begins with a planning guide that lists the two categories of attitudes and perceptions important to learning and the components of each (see Figure 2.1). While looking over the planning guide, she realizes that she can't attend to all these components in a single unit, so she lists the ones she will emphasize and the steps she will take to do so:

1. *Help students feel accepted by the teacher.* Greeting students at the door every day will help start classes on a positive note.

2. *Help students perceive classroom tasks as valuable.* Explaining how tasks might relate to students' daily lives will help students' develop a more positive attitude toward them. Ms. Conklin realizes that she must first find out what her students are interested in, but she thinks the extra effort will pay off.

3. *Help students be clear about classroom tasks.* Describing how each task might look when completed or presenting models of completed tasks will help students understand what they are trying to achieve.

As Ms. Conklin's example illustrates, planning for Dimension 1 is basically a matter of asking and answering two broad questions that include several more specific questions:

1. What will be done to help students develop positive attitudes and perceptions about the learning climate?

    a. What will be done to help students feel accepted by the teacher and by their peers?

    b. What will be done to help students perceive the classroom as a comfortable and orderly place?

2. What will be done to help students develop positive attitudes about classroom tasks?

    a. What will be done to help students perceive classroom tasks as valuable?

    b. What will be done to help students believe they can perform classroom tasks?

    c. What will be done to help students understand and be clear about classroom tasks?

FIGURE 2.1
Unit Planning Guide for
Dimension 1: Attitudes and Perceptions

CLASSROOM CLIMATE	CLASSROOM TASKS
What I will do to help students:	What I will do to help students:
✓ Feel accepted by the teacher and their peers	✓ Perceive classroom tasks as valuable
— Perceive the classroom as a comfortable and orderly place	— Believe they can perform the tasks
	✓ Understand and be clear about tasks
Activities Selected:	Activities Selected:
- Try to meet students at door and greet every day.	- Give an explanation and discuss how this info relates to them. - Try to describe or present a model of how each task should look when complete (regularly).

These questions cannot be addressed in every lesson. As Ms. Conklin's planning illustrates, only a few are emphasized in any one unit of instruction. Over the school year, though, a teacher would probably address all these questions. If a teacher consciously and systematically addresses one or more of the areas of Dimension 1, students will likely develop and maintain positive attitudes and perceptions about learning.

3

❖

DIMENSION 2
Acquiring and Integrating Knowledge

❖

A fundamental goal of schooling is for students to learn whatever
is deemed important in a given subject—in other words, to acquire
and integrate knowledge. There is a strong movement afoot to suggest,
wrongly I believe, that many educational innovations either ignore the
importance of content knowledge or actually work against it. Popular
books such as E. D. Hirsch's *Cultural Literacy: What Every American
Needs to Know* (1987), Alan Bloom's *The Closing of the American Mind*
(1987) and Diane Ravitch and Chester Finn's *What Do Our 17-Year-Olds
Know?* (1987) have directly or indirectly blamed the current emphasis
on teaching and reinforcing thinking processes (among other things) for
the perceived decline in test scores across the nation. Many reviewers
of these works, however, say that these are straw-man arguments. For
example, Farrell (1991) notes that the critical flaw in all three works is
that they generate a false dichotomy between teaching thinking processes and teaching content- or domain-specific knowledge. They also
tend to equate an emphasis on domain-specific knowledge with an
emphasis on factual knowledge. Farrell, commenting on the works of
Hirsch (1987) and Ravitch and Finn (1987), notes that the heavy
emphasis on factual recall found in both books would seem to lead
inexorably to increased teacher domination and prescriptiveness, thus
perpetuating a tradition that many people assert is crippling American
education (Goodlad 1984; Powell, Farrar, and Cohen 1985).

The belief underlying the Dimensions of Learning model is that both content knowledge and thinking and reasoning processes need to be taught if we want students to become proficient learners. As Glaser (1984, 1985) and Resnick (1987) point out, reasoning processes are an integral part of content knowledge. Moreover, an emphasis on content knowledge does not translate into an emphasis on factual knowledge. Although facts are important, they are often rather meaningless in isolation. As both *Project 2061* (AAAS 1989) and the "standards project" of the National Council of Teachers of Mathematics (NCTM 1989) affirm, facts are most relevant when they illustrate, reinforce, or make concrete some larger concept or principle.

There is no debate, then, about the importance of content knowledge nor is there an attempt to undermine it. There is, however, a growing body of research and theory identifying the most useful content knowledge and how to learn it.

How can educators best help students acquire and integrate knowledge? Before answering this question, recall the story of Miguel (in Chapter 1), who learned to perform the back kick in Mr. Tully's phys ed class. Learning the kick initially involved linking new information with old information. Miguel compared the back kick with the side kick that he already knew how to perform. Next, he had to work out some of the kinks and organize the information into simple steps. Finally, he had to internalize the information so that he could easily use it again. Miguel's story illustrates some of the basic dynamics of acquiring and integrating new knowledge, but to fully understand how we acquire knowledge, we need to consider the nature of knowledge itself.

The Nature of Knowledge

Noneducators tend to think all knowledge is pretty much the same. But many theorists believe there are different types of knowledge, each involving somewhat different learning processes. At the most basic and general level are the two categories of knowledge shown in columns A and B below.

A	B
reading a map	democracy
performing long division	a numerator
setting up an experiment	an amoeba
editing an essay	the conventions of punctuation
shooting a free throw	the rules of basketball

Column A contains examples of knowledge that involve processes. These processes may or may not be performed in a linear fashion. For example, performing long division is a process: You perform one step, then another, and so on. Reading a map also involves certain steps, but these steps, unlike those in long division, do not have to be performed in any set order. You might read the name of the map first, then look at the legend, or you might just as effectively perform these steps in reverse order. Knowledge of this sort is usually called *procedural knowledge*. You might think of it as the skills and processes important to a given content area.

The examples in column B do not involve a process or a set of steps. Acquiring this type of knowledge involves understanding the component parts and being able to recall them. For example, knowledge of the concept of "democracy" includes understanding that decisions are made by the people, each person has a single vote, votes are weighted equally, and so on. It also includes the ability to remember this information or at least recognize it at some later date. This type of knowledge is commonly called *declarative knowledge*.

What is important about these two types of knowledge is that they involve somewhat different learning processes (though both require the three general phases exemplified in Miguel's story). The distinction between the two types of knowledge is reflected in current efforts to define standards for what students should know *and* be able to do. Let's compare the examples below. Ms. Baker's class illustrates how procedural knowledge is learned, and Mr. DiStefano's class illustrates how declarative knowledge is learned.

Ms. Baker's Class

Ms. Baker is introducing her students to the process of three-column addition. She begins by telling them not to worry—what they are about to do is just like what they did with two-column addition. To calm her students' fears, she takes some time to review the steps of two-column addition. As she does so, she writes the steps on the board. Then she works on the board the problem 374 + 251, thinking aloud as she does so: "Let's see, I add the 1 and the 4 in the first column. That doesn't go over 10 so I don't have to carry anything over to the second column. Now I just add the numbers in the second column because I didn't have to carry anything. OK, the 7 and 5 add up to 12. If this were two-column addition, I'd just write the 12 down, but it's three-column addition so I have to consider the next column. Well, it's just like what I have to do with the first column of two-column addition. I have to carry over the 1 from the 12. Let's see, I bring the 1 over to the column that has the 3 and the 2; they add up to 5 plus the 1 that I carried from the second column. That's it, 625. That wasn't so hard. It's the same as two-column addition, only you have to think of carrying twice, not just once."

When Ms. Baker completes the problem, she adds the steps for three-column addition to those already on the board for two-column addition. She then reviews the steps for three-column addition by performing one more example, pointing out each step as she goes through the problem. Students then pair up and work on two practice problems she has given them. She tells them to take their time and think through every step. When pairs are done, Ms. Baker works the problems on the board with the entire class, pointing out each step.

The next day, she works another problem on the board. With this one, however, she asks the class questions as she goes along: "What would happen if this were a 7 instead of a 4? Would I have to carry or not? How small a number would have to be here for me not to have to carry? What happens if I don't have to carry in the second column but I do in the first and the third? Show me an example. What happens if I've had to carry in the second and third columns but not the first? Show me."

It seems as though Ms. Baker is trying to cover every possible situation that might occur with three-column addition and, in fact, she is. She is trying to expose students to as many variations as possible. She is also trying to point out common kinds of mistakes. It takes her more than fifteen minutes to go through a single problem and all its variations. She then gives the class more problems to solve. Again, students do them in pairs. The students very quickly discover that these problems involve all the "tricky parts" and variations Ms. Baker just covered. Even though the problems are tough, the students do well. As they work on the problems, Ms. Baker walks around the room, helping them with the difficult parts and making sure both students in each pair understand the many variations she has reviewed.

Over the next few days, Ms. Baker gives more problems on three-column addition. She gradually begins to emphasize speed, but she never stops emphasizing the understanding of each step. Within a week, students in her class have become proficient solvers of three-column addition problems.

Mr. DiStefano's Class

Mr. DiStefano is introducing a new chapter on alcohol in health class. He begins by asking students what they already know about the topic. Being a typical group of 11th graders, they begin with statements like "It's OK for adults but they won't let us have any" and "It's fun." Mr. DiStefano records their remarks on the board as students call them out. After a few minutes, the class starts providing more "academic" responses: "It's addictive." "It ruins your life."

After students have generated about ten ideas, Mr. DiStefano gives each student a piece of paper divided into two columns. In the left column is the phrase "Effects of Alcohol on the Body" and in the right column is the phrase "Effects of Alcohol on Behavior." Mr. DiStefano asks his students to read the chapter and add items to each column as they do so. He says, "By the time you are done reading the chapter you should have at least five things listed under each heading."

The students begin reading. It's a short chapter, so in about fifteen minutes everyone is finished. Mr. DiStefano then says, "Let's see what you've come up with." As a class, they go over the information in their outlines, and Mr. DiStefano makes a large graphic representation of the information. At the top of the graph, he writes, "Alcohol is a very powerful drug." Under that he writes the two areas he asked students to attend to, "Effects of Alcohol on the Body" and "Effects of Alcohol on Behavior." As students call out what they have identified, Mr. DiStefano lists the information under the appropriate heading.

When they finish the list, Mr. DiStefano says that he would like everyone to remember a few of the items they've listed. He then puts a check mark next to the pieces of information he considers particularly important. To help students remember the marked information, he tells a story about someone he once knew who drank too much alcohol. The students love the story because Mr. DiStefano makes it realistic. He describes sounds, smells, tastes, and emotions. It's almost like watching a movie. By the time he's finished, he's covered all the pieces of information he checked off on the board.

In her class, Ms. Baker was helping students learn a new skill, three-column addition. Because it involves steps or rules to follow—in this case, rules that must be applied in a relatively strict order—this is a type of procedural knowledge. Learning procedural knowledge involves three phases that researchers usually call the cognitive, associative, and autonomous phases (Anderson 1982, 1983; Fitts and Posner 1967). In the Dimensions of Learning framework they have somewhat different names that highlight specific aspects of each phase.

The first thing Ms. Baker did was to help students identify what they already knew about three-column addition by likening it to two-column addition. She did this because the first step in learning any new skill or process is to establish a rough model of it—to get an idea of what the skill or process involves. Consequently, we call the first phase of learning procedural knowledge *model construction*. At this stage the learner cannot actually perform the skill; he simply has an idea of the steps involved. For example, when I first learned how to drive I took time to memorize the position of the gears, and I created a model of the process of shifting into the various gears that I would frequently rehearse in my mind—even though I had never actually tried it.

After students had a rough model of the process, Ms. Baker engaged them in an in-depth analysis of it. Using a single example, she showed several variations of the process and pointed out some common pitfalls. This is called the *shaping* phase of learning procedural knowledge. It is probably the most crucial part of learning a new skill or process because without it errors can easily creep into the new procedure. As we shall see, many of these errors can go unnoticed by even the most discerning teacher.

Finally, Ms. Baker set up a practice schedule for students. The intent here was for students to focus on speed and accuracy and develop their skill at three-column addition to a point where they could solve problems without thinking about each step involved. This is called the *internalizing* phase to emphasize that skills and processes are most useful when they are learned to such an extent that they can be done with little conscious effort.

Whereas Ms. Baker was helping students acquire and integrate procedural knowledge, Mr. DiStefano was helping students acquire and integrate declarative knowledge: specific facts and pieces of information about alcohol. Here, too, there were three phases of learning. At first, Mr. DiStefano asked students what they already knew about alcohol. The purpose of this activity was to help students *construct meaning*: to associate what they already knew about alcohol with the new information they were reading about alcohol. The first step in learning declarative knowledge is to link new knowledge with old knowledge. It's a rather curious paradox in learning theory that we have to know something about what we are learning to learn it well. But if you stop to think about it, we are constantly using what we know to help us figure out what we don't know.

The second phase of learning declarative knowledge is an *organizational* phase. Here the learner arranges the new information to create some meaningful pattern. In this case, Mr. DiStefano helped his students by giving them a graphic organizer. This phase is similar to the shaping phase of learning procedural knowledge. It involves honing information down to the necessary ingredients and identifying important relationships among pieces of information.

Finally, Mr. DiStefano helped students *store* the information in their long-term memory. This is the final phase of learning declarative knowledge: overtly representing information in long-term memory in a way that makes it easy to remember later. Mr. DiStefano helped students create mental pictures of the information by telling them a story about a friend.

Helping students acquire and integrate basic declarative and procedural knowledge requires attention to the three aspects of learning specific to each type of knowledge. Because much of the content students encounter in schools is declarative in nature, we will consider declarative knowledge first.

Helping Students Learn Declarative Knowledge

Learning declarative knowledge involves three phases: constructing meaning, organizing, and storing. We will explore each of these phases and discuss a few strategies for helping students move through the three phases.

Constructing Meaning for Declarative Knowledge

The driving force behind constructing meaning is using what we already know about a topic to interpret what we are learning. Without prior knowledge with which to interpret new declarative knowledge, nothing makes much sense. From a learning perspective, it is impossible to overestimate the importance of using prior knowledge to interpret new information. Bartlett (1932) illustrated this when he asked British readers to discuss a story from the oral tradition of a tribe of Indians on the west coast of Canada. The story fit well with the Indians' view of the world or their "schema" for how the world works. It made sense to them. It did not, however, make much sense to the British readers, whose view of the world was quite different from the Indians'. The British readers saw the story quite differently. The story Bartlett used is printed on the next page. Read it and see if it makes any sense to you.

The War of the Ghosts

One night two young men from Egulac went down to the river to hunt seals, and while they were there it became foggy and calm. Then they heard war-cries, and they thought: "Maybe this is a war-party." They escaped to the shore, and hid behind a log. Now canoes came up, and they heard the noise of paddles, and saw one canoe coming up to them. There were five men in the canoe, and they said:

"What do you think? We wish to take you along. We are going up the river to make war on the people."

One of the young men said, "I have no arrows."

"Arrows are in the canoe," they said.

"I will not go along. I might be killed. My relatives do not know where I have gone. But you," he said, turning to the other, "may go with them."

So one of the young men went, but the other returned home.

And the warriors went on up the river to a town on the other side of Kalama. The people came down to the water, and they began to fight, and many were killed. But presently the young man heard one of the warriors say: "Quick, let us go home: that Indian has been hit." Now he thought: "Oh, they are ghosts." He did not feel sick, but they said he had been shot.

So the canoes went back to Egulac, and the young man went ashore to his house, and made a fire. And he told everybody and said: "Behold I accompanied the ghosts, and we went to fight. Many of our fellows were killed, and many of those who attacked us were killed. They said I was hit, and I did not feel sick."

He told it all, and then he became quiet. When the sun rose he fell down. Something black came out of his mouth. His face became contorted. The people jumped up and cried.

He was dead (Anderson 1990, p. 196).

The story probably seems bizarre to you. It certainly did to Bartlett's readers, who were products of upper-class Edwardian England. In fact, Bartlett found that his readers actually had to change what they read to understand it. As Anderson (1990, p. 197) notes, they distorted the story to fit their own cultural stereotypes. For instance, "something black came from his mouth" in the original story translated to "he frothed at the mouth" or "he vomited."

The power of our background knowledge to influence what we perceive was also demonstrated in a study by Brewer and Treyens (1981). They brought thirty subjects, individually, into a room and told them that it was the office of the experimenter and that they were to wait there for a short time. After thirty-five seconds, the subjects were taken to another room and asked to write down everything they could recall about the office. Brewer and Treyens' hypothesis was that the subjects would recall items that were part of the standard schema for a psychologist's office, but not recall very many items that did not fit their schema for a psychologist's office. And this was, in fact, what they found. Specifically, twenty-nine of thirty subjects remembered that the office had a desk and a chair, but only eight recalled that it had a bulletin board or a skull. And nine subjects recalled that the office had books, which it did not.

Constructing meaning using prior knowledge, then, is a vital component of learning declarative knowledge. A number of strategies can facilitate this process. Such strategies basically help learners access what they already know about information, use it to make predictions about what they are learning, and then confirm or disconfirm their initial guesses. One of the most popular strategies is the K-W-L strategy developed by Donna Ogle (1986). During the first phase of the strategy, students identify what they think they **K**now about the topic. For example, before reading a chapter describing how lakes die, students would list the facts they already know about this phenomenon. Next, they would list what they **W**ant to know about the topic: interesting questions that have come to mind as a result of identifying what they think they know. For the topic of dying lakes, students might ask these questions: How long does it take for a lake to die? What exactly is the process? Can dead lakes be revived?

Students then read the chapter with an eye toward answering the questions they have posed. The last step in the K-W-L process is for students to identify what they have **L**earned. Here students record the answers to their questions as well as other information they have learned. In many cases, they also find out that what they thought they knew was inaccurate.

Another powerful strategy for the constructing meaning phase of learning declarative knowledge is the concept formation strategy described by Joyce and Weil (1986) and based on the research of Bruner, Goodnow, and Austin (1956). In the process described by Joyce and Weil (and adaptations of it), students are initially presented with examples and nonexamples of a new concept. To illustrate, if a teacher wanted to help students acquire the concept of "an adjective," she might first present students with the following examples and nonexamples:

Example: Our *triumphant* team came home after the game.

Nonexample: We were happy about our *triumph*.

Example: He fixed the *broken* chair.

Nonexample: He sank into the *chair*.

Example: The *bright* light hurt my eyes.

Nonexample: He listened *attentively*.

As the teacher presents these examples and nonexamples, students try to determine the critical attributes of the concept being formed. In situations like this, learners commonly devise a model containing hypothetical characteristics and then use each new example and nonexample to test the validity of that model. After one round of examples and nonexamples is presented, students are given time to reflect on the model they have generated. Another set of examples and nonexamples is provided to allow students to further test their models. At the end of this round, students share their model with the rest of the class so that a composite model can be built. More examples and nonexamples are provided to test this composite model. Students are then asked to find or create their own examples and nonexamples for a final round of testing. The concept is then named and a definition constructed by the group. The last activity in the process is for students to describe the reasoning they used during the concept formation process.

Strategies for helping students construct meaning for declarative knowledge are many and varied. Brainstorming, analogizing, semantic webbing, and reciprocal teaching are a few that teachers might use. The important point of any of these strategies is that before exposing students to new content, teachers overtly help each learner tap into his or her prior knowledge and use that knowledge to guide understanding and comprehension.

Organizing Declarative Knowledge

You might think that constructing meaning is all there is to acquiring and integrating declarative knowledge. But another process is necessary for learners to truly make the information their own. In the Dimensions of Learning model, this process is called "organizing." At a very basic level, organizing involves representing information in a subjective way. It includes identifying what is important and not important and then generating a semantic or symbolic representation of that information.

Walter Kintsch and Teun van Dijk have been particularly influential in helping us understand this process. In a series of studies (Kintsch 1974, 1979; Kintsch and van Dijk 1978; van Dijk 1977, 1980; van Dijk and Kintsch 1983), they have shown that we create our own internal representation (a macrostructure) of the information we comprehend (a microstructure). We do this by replacing specific pieces of information with more general ones. For example, if we read that "the dog named Spot picked up the tennis ball," we might construct our macrostructure using the phrase "the dog picked up a ball."

We often unconsciously summarize large sets of specific information and thus tend to remember the gist of information rather than specifics. To confirm this for yourself, try writing down the details of a movie you saw a week ago. Then take your written account and watch the movie again. You'll find that you probably remembered the general theme of the movie but forgot many details. This is because you created a macrostructure of the movie; you organized the information in the movie in a subjective, concise way.

Perhaps the most obvious strategy for helping learners organize information is to use advance organizers, as described by Ausubel (1968). These usually take the form of questions provided to students before they read a section in a textbook, watch a film, or complete some other activity. The questions guide students in organizing the information they will encounter. Some other ways of helping students organize information include using physical and symbolic representations, using organizational patterns, and using graphic organizers.

USING PHYSICAL AND SYMBOLIC REPRESENTATIONS

The most basic type of organizational representation is physical or symbolic. As the name implies, a physical representation is a physical model of the information. For example, in a science class students might create a physical model of the solar system using materials like plastic balls and wire. They would also be creating a physical model if they "acted out" the parts of the solar system (as in the class described in Chapter 1). Physical models include any three-dimensional representation of information. The emphasis is on a realistic image of the component parts.

Symbolic representations are not intended to be as realistic as physical representations. Let's use the following equation as an example:

$$F = \frac{(M^1, M^2)G}{r^2}$$

The equation states that force (F) is equal to the product of the masses of two objects (M_1 and M_2) times a constant G divided by the square of the distance between them (r). With this explanation, you might understand the equation at the level of constructed meaning, but to truly understand it you would have to create a symbolic representation that allows you to internalize the relationships among the various quantities. Hayes (1981) suggests an image of two large globes in space with the learner in the middle trying to hold them apart:

> If either of the globes were very heavy, we would expect that it would be harder to hold them apart, than if both were light. Since force increases as either of the masses (M's) increases, the masses must be in the numerator. As we push the globes further apart, the force of attraction between them will decrease as the force of attraction between two magnets decreases as we pull them apart. Since force decreases as distance increases, r must be in the denominator (p. 126).

Physical and symbolic representations, then, force the learner to recast information to make salient important information and relationships.

USING ORGANIZATIONAL PATTERNS

Over the last twenty years, researchers in the field of discourse analysis have demonstrated that a great deal of declarative knowledge can be organized in various types of semantic patterns. Combining the work of Cooper (1983), Frederiksen (1977), and Meyer (1975) yields at least six general organizational patterns:

• *Descriptive patterns* organize facts or characteristics about specific persons, places, things, and events. The facts or characteristics need be in no particular order. For example, information in a film about the Empire State building—its height, when it was built, how many rooms it has, and so on—might be organized as a simple descriptive pattern.

• *Sequence patterns* organize events in a specific chronological order. For example, a chapter in a book relating the events that occurred between John F. Kennedy's assassination on November 22, 1963, and his burial on November 25, 1963, might be organized as a sequence pattern.

• *Process/Cause patterns* organize information into a causal network leading to a specific outcome or into a sequence of steps leading to a specific product. For example, information about the events leading to the Civil War might be organized as a process/cause pattern.

• *Problem/Solution patterns* organize information into an identified problem and its possible solutions. For example, information about the various types of diction errors that might occur in an essay and the ways of correcting those errors might be organized as a problem/solution pattern.

• *Generalization patterns* organize information into a generalization with supporting examples. For example, a chapter in a textbook about U.S. presidents might be organized using this generalization: "U.S. presidents frequently come from influential families." It would be followed by examples of specific presidents.

• *Concept patterns* organize general categories or classes of persons, places, things, or events. Concept patterns usually include the defining characteristics and specific examples of the concept. For example, a film on the concept of "U.S. presidents" might contain defining characteristics of this concept, such as "they are elected by the citizens," and specific examples of presidents.

Students can use any one of these six patterns to organize information when they listen to a lecture, read a book, watch a film, and so on. Figure 3.1, for example, shows information adapted from a social studies textbook. Students might organize this information as a description of specific events that occurred in Italy and Germany before World War II. Or they might organize the information as defining characteristics about the general concept of "dictators," along with the specific examples of Mussolini and Hitler. Finally, they might organize the information as examples of the generalization "Dictators can easily rise to power in countries that are experiencing severe economic depression." With the aid of a few basic organizational structures, this one piece of expository information can be organized in several ways.

USING GRAPHIC ORGANIZERS

Using graphic organizers to outline information is very popular in the classroom. Examples of how graphic organizers can be used across different content areas have been offered by Jones, Palincsar, Ogle, and Carr (1987), Heimlich and Pittelman (1988), McTighe and Lyman (1988), and Clarke (1991). Using different types of graphic representations to organize information is tantamount to using different organizational patterns. Figure 3.2 shows a graphic representation for each of the six types of organizational patterns described earlier.

If students wanted to organize the information in Figure 3.1 as a generalization about dictators, they might use a graphic representation like that in Figure 3.3 (on page 46).

FIGURE 3.1
Information from a Social Studies Text

The United States was not the only nation to suffer from the Great Depression. The nations of Europe also were hard hit. Moreover, many Europeans had been trying to repair the damage to their countries caused during World War I.

Because of the hardships under which they were forced to live, some Europeans were willing to listen to leaders who promised to make their nations rich and powerful again. Some of these leaders brought about total changes in their countries. Their actions also caused another world war.

Dictators rise to power. In the 1920's and 1930's new leaders formed governments in Italy, Germany, and Japan. The governments formed in these countries were *dictatorships*. In a dictatorship, the leader or leaders hold complete authority over the people they rule. The people living in a dictatorship have only those rights that their leader, the dictator, chooses to give them. Dictators alone make all the important decisions in their nations. The decisions made by the dictators of Italy, Germany, and Japan led to World War II.

Mussolini takes over in Italy. After World War I, many Italians wanted to feel pride in the strength of their country once again. Benito Mussolini, the founder and organizer of the Fascist Party, convinced the Italians that he and his party could strengthen the nation. To succeed, the Fascists had to take control of the economy, the government, and many other parts of Italian life.

In 1922, the Fascists took control of the Italian government, creating a dictatorship with Mussolini as leader. Italians who were against Mussolini or his government were either thrown into prison or were forced to leave the country.

Mussolini planned to increase Italy's power and wealth by taking over weaker nations. He turned to Africa and, in 1935, attacked Ethiopia. Within a few weeks the Italian army overran this East African country and added it to the Italian empire.

Hitler becomes dictator in Germany. After losing World War I, Germany continued to struggle with severe economic problems throughout the 1920's. These difficulties and the memory of their defeat in World War I brought many Germans to the Nazi Party. Its leader, Adolf Hitler, promised to make Germany the most powerful country in the world. In 1933 the Nazis won control of the German government. Hitler became Germany's dictator and silenced anyone who opposed him.

The people against whom Hitler directed his greatest hatred were the Jewish citizens of Germany. He unfairly blamed them for all of Germany's problems. By constantly repeating these false accusations, Hitler aroused public opinion in Germany against its Jewish citizens. Then he took away all civil rights and property of the Jews. Next, the police rounded up Jewish men, women, and children and sent them into *concentration camps*, or prison camps.

Hitler promised the Germans that he would add to the territory of their nation. He immediately put the country to work making weapons and other war materials. The first nation he moved into was Austria, in 1938. Hitler annexed Austria, he explained, because most of its people were Germans.

Source: Marzano 1991. Copyright© 1991 by National Council of Teachers of English. Reprinted by permission.

FIGURE 3.2
Six Types of Graphic Organizers

Descriptive Pattern

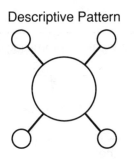

Sequence Pattern

Process/Cause Pattern

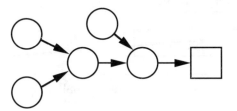

Problem/Solution Pattern

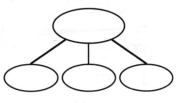

Generalization Pattern

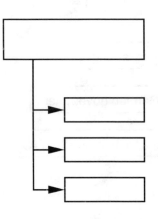

Concept Pattern

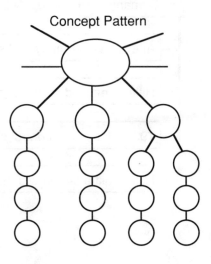

FIGURE 3.3
A Graphic Representation of a Generalization
About Dictators

Dictators rise to power when countries are weak by promising them strength.

In Italy . . .

Italians wanted to feel proud about their country.

Mussolini convinced them that he and Fascists would take control of the country and make it strong.

1922: Fascists created a dictatorship.

Mussolini sought power by taking over weaker nations.

In Germany . . .

After WWI Germany had severe problems.

Hitler promised to make the country strong.

1933: Nazis won control of the German government.

Hitler built a strong war machine and then attacked Austria.

If students wanted to organize that same information around the concept of dictators, they might use the graphic representation shown in Figure 3.4.

Again, the same information can be organized in a variety of ways using a variety of formats. Remember that organizing information is a somewhat subjective process in which the learner structures information in ways unique to her perspective. She highlights some ideas, makes others subordinate, and even disregards a few.

FIGURE 3.4
A Graphic Representation of the Concept of Dictators

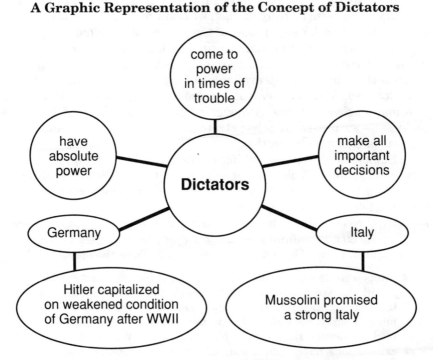

Storing Declarative Knowledge

Storage strategies would be unnecessary if learners didn't have to remember information over an extended period of time. Being able to recall some information, however, is vital for success in all content areas; imagine, for example, how difficult much of mathematics would be if you couldn't remember the times tables. There is growing national pressure for students to recall more and more factual information. Witness Ravitch and Finn's (1987) review of 141 specific pieces of information in assessing how much American 17-year-olds know about literature and history. Indeed, Doyle (1983) asserts that recall of information is still the primary task required of students.

Cognitive psychologists have taught us a lot about storing information in long-term memory. In fact, we know more about how information can be stored for easy retrieval than we do about almost any other aspect of learning. Unfortunately, what we know is usually not taught in the classroom. Most students use only verbal rehearsal, perhaps the weakest of all the strategies available, to help them remember what they have learned. Verbal rehearsal involves saying, reading, or writing information several times. Although verbal rehearsal works, its effectiveness is surpassed by other strategies, all of which fall under the general category of elaboration.

Elaboration involves making many and varied linkages between new information and old. An experiment by Owens, Bower, and Black (1979) illustrates the working principles underlying elaboration. Subjects studied a story that followed the principal character, a college student, through a day in her life: making a cup of coffee in the morning, visiting a doctor, attending a lecture, shopping for groceries, and attending a cocktail party. The following is a passage from the story:

> Nancy went to see the doctor. She arrived at the office and checked in with the receptionist. She went to see the nurse who went through the usual procedures. Then Nancy stepped on the scale and the nurse recorded her weight. The doctor entered the room and examined the results. He smiled at Nancy and said, "Well, it seems my expectations have been confirmed." When the examination was finished, Nancy left the office.

Two groups of subjects studied the story. The only difference between the groups was that the "theme group" had been told that Nancy had been feeling nauseated when she woke up in the morning and was wondering if she was pregnant.

The researchers hypothesized that the subjects who had the extra information would develop a theme about Nancy that would automatically stimulate elaboration. When subjects in both groups were asked to recall the information twenty-four hours later, those in the theme group recalled it in significantly more detail. Those in the "neutral group" recalled very little. Elaborating on the information they had been given helped the subjects in the theme group store the information in an easily retrievable manner.

Virtually all memorization techniques use some form of elaboration. One of the most powerful ways to elaborate on information is to imagine mental pictures, physical sensations, and emotions associated with the information. Mr. DiStefano was helping students elaborate on the information about alcohol when he told the story of the person he knew who drank too much. As he described sounds, smells, tastes, and so on, he was helping students create images that were elaborations on the basic information about alcohol.

Many formal memory systems use imagery as an elaboration tool. Two of these are the rhyming pegword system (Miller, Galanter, and Pribram 1960) and the method of "places" or loci (Ross and Lawrence 1968), both of which are described in detail by Hayes (1981) and Lindsay and Norman (1977). One of the most commonly used imagery strategies is the "link technique." Here, the learner creates a mental image for each piece of information he wants to recall, making sure to create vivid patterns by imagining sounds, tastes, smells, and so on. He then links the separate images in story fashion.

For example, if a student used the link technique to store the information about dictators, he would first form an image of a dictator, perhaps using Saddam Hussein as that image. As he formed the image, he would try to incorporate touch, feel, smell, sound, and emotion. To remember that dictators rise to power when countries are weakened by promising them strength, the student might imagine Saddam in a city that is in grave disrepair, where buildings are falling down and people are starving. The dictator would be making a speech promising that he will make the city strong again. As the dictator makes the speech, he might become larger and larger until he towers above the skyline. To link the information about Hitler, the student might then imagine Adolf Hitler walking into the scene and shaking hands with Saddam Hussein, and so on. In short, the student creates elaborated images and then "chains" them together in story fashion.

Planning for the Acquisition and Integration of Declarative Knowledge

Planning instruction that will help students learn declarative knowledge is one of the most difficult tasks a teacher faces, because most of what students read, hear, and experience in any unit of instruction is declarative in nature. Consequently, the teacher must sift through the information students will be exposed to and make important decisions about how students will construct meaning and then organize and store that information. Let's look at how Ms. Conklin approaches this task.

Ms. Conklin's Planning for Dimension 2: Declarative Knowledge

Ms. Conklin is planning a unit on weather. Although she has a general sense of what she wants students to know at the end of four weeks, she hasn't really thought through the specifics. She starts by identifying some general topics. She knows that she'd like students to understand something about tornadoes and weather forecasting because tornadoes occur frequently in the region. She also wants students to have a general idea of how weather affects our lives. She records these general topics in a unit planning guide (see column 1 of Figure 3.5 on page 51).

If Ms. Conklin knew all about weather forecasting, tornadoes, and the effects of weather, she could identify the specific pieces of information included in each of these general topics. But when she asks herself, "What exactly should students know?" she realizes that *she* doesn't really know, so she decides to investigate the topics further. She starts by looking through the textbook and finds information about all three topics. She also reads a few articles in the encyclopedia, looks through some filmstrips at the library, talks to the weather forecaster from Channel 9, talks to a meteorologist at the university, and even visits the forecasting center at the university. She's amazed at how much information she has to collect just to answer this one question.

For the topic of forecasting weather, Ms. Conklin decides that students should know about barometers and thermometers and the rise and drop in air pressure. For the topic of tornadoes, she concludes that students should know the sequence of events that leads to the formation of a tornado. Finally, for the topic of how weather affects our life, she thinks students should realize that weather influences us in many ways every

FIGURE 3.5
Unit Planning Guide for
Dimension 2: Acquiring and Integrating Declarative Knowledge

Topics	What are the specifics?	How will information be experienced—directly or indirectly?	How will students be aided in constructing meaning?	How will students be aided in organizing information?	How will students be aided in storing information?
Forecasting weather	• Barometer • Thermometer Cause/effect of rise/drop in air pressure	• Textbook PP. 15-18 • Filmstrip Guest lecturer from Channel 9	• Students will brainstorm before reading • K-W-L Guest will use analogy	I will provide set of questions to be used for both activities I will provide graphic organizer	I will guide students thru mental pictures, sensations, etc.
Tornadoes	Sequence of events from formation to disappearance	• Textbook PP. 21-25 • Field trip to university forecasting center	Students will develop set of questions to use for both	Students will create graphic organizers from responses to questions	Students will create their own mental pictures, sensations, etc.
Weather affects us	Weather affects us daily, directly and indirectly – economy – history – recreation – moods	• Read article "Weather and War" • Film – "Partly Cloudy, Cold," and Humid	• Before, During, After Strategy • Brainstorm effects of weather	Students will build a class collage graphically organized around generalization	

day. She records these specifics in the planning guide (see column 2 of Figure 3.5).

Now that she has identified the specific information she wants students to learn, she concentrates on deciding what learning experiences she will use in the classroom. She begins with the information about weather forecasting. She decides that students will read pages 15–18 in the textbook to initially learn about barometers and thermometers. They will also watch a filmstrip. And she has invited the weather forecaster from Channel 9 to talk about air pressure. She records all these decisions in the planning guide (see column 3 of Figure 3.5).

Ms. Conklin also plans how students will be aided in constructing meaning for each of the three learning experiences she has identified. She decides to use brainstorming for the pages in the textbook, the K-W-L strategy for the filmstrip, and an analogy for the lecture. These decisions are also recorded in the planning guide (see column 4 of Figure 3.5).

For each of the learning experiences, Ms. Conklin also thinks about activities that will help students organize information. For the textbook and film, she decides that she will provide advance organizer questions, and with the guest lecture, she will provide students with a graphic organizer (see column 5 of Figure 3.5).

Ms. Conklin's final decision is about storing information. As she thinks about strategies, she concludes that she is not so concerned that students remember the information about barometers and thermometers, but she does want them to remember the information about air pressure. To help students store the information in a way that will help them recall it easily, she will guide them through the creation of mental pictures, physical sensations, and emotions about that information (see column 6 of Figure 3.5).

The set of decisions made, Ms. Conklin goes through the same process for the specific information about tornadoes and the effects of weather. The whole planning process has taken Ms. Conklin a lot longer than she anticipated, but she feels very good about what she has done. She has established a strong direction for her unit on weather.

As this example illustrates, a teacher must consider several fundamental questions when planning instruction for Dimension 2, acquiring and integrating declarative knowledge:

1. What are the general topics? Identifying general topics makes good curricular sense because, as noted earlier, most of the major curriculum efforts in the content areas are focusing on themes that embrace "big ideas." For example, the California K–12 science framework identifies broad themes such as *energy, evolution,* and *patterns of change* (California State Board of Education 1990). The Bradley Commission's report on history in the schools (Gagnon and the Bradley Commission 1988) and *Project 2061: Science for All Americans* (AAAS 1989) place similar emphases on broad topics.

Teachers should not select topics arbitrarily. They should think carefully about the possible reasons for selecting topics:

- The topics are important to the general culture.
- They are important to the community.
- They are of interest to students.
- They are of interest to the teacher.
- They will be useful at a later date.
- They are specified by the district or state.
- They are topics for which resources are readily available.

2. What are the specifics? Within any general topic are numerous specific areas that can be focused on. Students should have some freedom and flexibility to focus on the information they consider important, but educators have a responsibility to provide guidance about the important information within a general topic. This guidance is the heart of the "heritage model" of schooling, which says that it is the duty of the education community to help society maintain a common culture by passing on specific information to students (Farrell 1991). Although there are some efforts at the national level to identify these specifics (e.g., Ravitch and Finn 1987), making such decisions at the local level seems to be a more valid practice. It makes far more sense for individual teachers like Ms. Conklin to decide which specifics to emphasize so that adjustments can be made to account for individual student needs and interests and the culture of the local community.

Regardless of who makes the decision, at this level of planning it is important not to equate identifying specifics with identifying facts. Klausmeier and his colleagues (Klausmeier 1985, Klausmeier and Sipple 1980, Katz 1976) have illustrated that large cognitive structures are more robust learning constructs than facts. Focusing on concepts and generalization naturally organizes the facts that support them, making the information easier to understand and recall.

3. How will students experience the information? One of the most important decisions a teacher can make about declarative information is how students will experience it. In a very general sense, there are two ways that students can experience declarative information, directly or indirectly, as depicted in Figure 3.6.

A direct experience, as the name implies, involves physical activity by students. This physical involvement can be real or simulated. For example, a real, direct experience for students studying the topic of democracy would be one that involved students in a democratic activity. The teacher might have students use the democratic process to make all classroom decisions during a two-week period. Unfortunately, not all classroom content can be experienced directly in a real way. For instance, students cannot learn about hibernation by experiencing it directly because hibernation is physically impossible for human beings. They can simulate the experience, though, by lying very still for ten minutes and consciously trying to slow their heartbeat and their breathing.

FIGURE 3.6
Ways to Experience Declarative Information

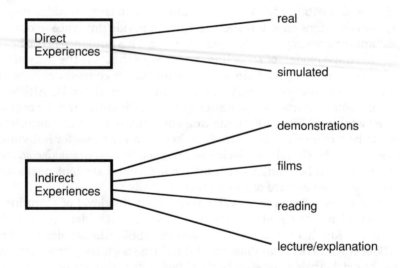

Indirect experiences are those in which students are not physically involved. Demonstrations, films, readings, and lectures are all indirect experiences. Some indirect ways of learning about hibernation would be observing a classroom pet that goes into hibernation for the winter, watching a film on hibernation, reading about hibernation, or listening to an oral presentation about hibernation.

I often use Figure 3.6 when I ask teachers to rate their use of various types of direct and indirect experiences. Lecture and reading are the most common experiences used, primarily because they require the least amount of time and preparation. If at all possible, though, teachers should attempt to vary the ways students experience content. For example, in Ms. Conklin's unit on weather, students will have the indirect experiences of reading, watching films and filmstrips, and listening to lectures. They will also have the direct experience of visiting the weather forecasting center at the university and getting some hands-on use of the equipment. Over the course of the school year, every teacher should be able to use at least some direct experiences and to frequently use indirect experiences other than lecture and reading.

4. How will students be aided in constructing meaning? Given the importance of constructing meaning, teachers should use overt activities with every learning experience to aid students in this process. As Figure 3.5 on page 51 shows, Ms. Conklin has decided to use a variety of techniques, including brainstorming, questioning, and the K-W-L strategy.

5. How will students be aided in organizing the information? A key aspect of this decision is how much guidance the teacher will provide. Given the constructive nature of learning, it's important that students create their own organizational schemes. But if certain ways of organizing information are important, then students need guidance. Consequently, a balance of organizing activities, some directed by the teacher and some by students, is usually appropriate. Note that in some situations Ms. Conklin has decided to provide students with an organizational schema; in others, she has decided to have students direct the organizing process (see Column 5 of Figure 3.5).

6. How will students be aided in storing the information? Every unit of instruction contains an immense amount of declarative information, and teachers cannot expect students to remember all of it. Some information, though, might be considered important enough for the use of overt storage activities. As Figure 3.5 indicates, Ms. Conklin has decided that she will guide students through storage activities for the information about air pressure and the formation of a tornado. In one case, she will provide the mental pictures, physical sensations, and so on, to elaborate on the information. In the other, she will ask students to create their own elaborations.

Helping Students Learn Procedural Knowledge

Learning procedural knowledge involves three phases: constructing models, shaping, and internalizing. As with declarative knowledge, we will explore each of these phases and outline some ways you can help students move through the three phases.

Constructing Models for Procedural Knowledge

To understand the role of model building in procedural learning, it is important to understand the three basic types of procedures that might be taught in a content area class: algorithms, tactics, and strategies. *Algorithms* are sets of steps that guarantee a certain result (Anderson 1990, p. 226). For example, the procedure for multiplication is commonly thought of as an algorithm because it involves a series of steps that, when followed, will always result in a correct answer. *Tactics* are somewhat different. According to Snowman and McCown (1984), tactics aid in the accomplishment of a goal but do not necessarily ensure its accomplishment. They involve general rules rather than a series of steps. For example, the general rules for reading a bar graph are more tactical than algorithmic in nature. They don't ensure success in reading a bar graph, but they increase the probability of success. *Strategies,* unlike algorithms and tactics, are not specific to any one task. You would have a tactic for accomplishing the specific task of reading a bar graph, whereas you would have a general strategy for approaching problems of any type. Larkin (1981) found that experts in any field are far more strategic in their thinking than nonexperts in that field.

The initial models a learner builds, then, are somewhat different for each of the three types of procedures. The model for an algorithm would be a series of steps to be performed in a specific order: first you do this, then you do this, and so on. The model for a tactic would be a set of general rules (sometimes referred to as *heuristics*) that have a general rather than rigid order of application. The model for a strategy would be an even more general set of rules or heuristics that are not specific to one task. Although the initial models for algorithms, tactics, and strategies are somewhat different, the instructional techniques for helping students construct models for the procedures are the same. Among the most powerful techniques are analogizing, think-aloud modeling, and flow charting.

Analogizing is the process of providing students with an analogy that will help them construct an initial model of an algorithm, tactic, or strategy. The power of using analogy to help students understand a procedure was demonstrated in an experiment by Gick and Holyoak (1980). They presented their subjects with the following problem (which was adapted from Duncker 1945).

> Suppose you are a doctor faced with a patient who has a malignant tumor in his stomach. It is impossible to operate on the patient, but unless the tumor is destroyed the patient will die. There is a kind of ray that can be used to destroy the tumor. If the rays reach the tumor all at once at a sufficiently high intensity, the tumor will be destroyed. Unfortunately, at this intensity, the healthy tissue that the rays pass through on the way to the tumor will also be destroyed. At lower intensities the rays are harmless to healthy tissue, but they will not affect the tumor either. What type of procedure might be used to destroy the tumor with the rays, and at the same time avoid destroying the healthy tissue? (Gick and Holyoak 1980, pp. 307–308).

Few subjects were able to solve this problem when it was first presented because they had no process (tactic) to follow. Gick and Holyoak then presented their subjects with an analogy for the solution:

> A small country was ruled from a strong fortress by a dictator. The fortress was situated in the middle of the country, surrounded by farms and villages. Many roads led to the fortress through the countryside. A rebel general vowed to capture the fortress. The general knew that an attack by his entire army would capture the fortress. He gathered his army at the head of one of the roads, ready to launch a full-scale direct attack. However, the general then learned that the dictator had planted mines on each of the roads. The mines were set so that small bodies of men could pass over them safely, since the dictator needed to move his troops and workers to and from the fortress. However, any large force would detonate the mines. Not only would this blow up the road, but it would also destroy many neighboring villages. It therefore seemed impossible to capture the fortress. However, the general devised a simple plan. He divided his army into small groups and dispatched each group to the head of a different road. When all was ready he gave the signal and each group marched down a different road. Each group continued down its road to the fortress so that the entire army arrived together at the fortress at the same time. In this way, the general captured the fortress and overthrew the dictator (p. 351).

With this story as a hint, nearly all of the subjects were able to construct a tactic that allowed them to solve the problem.

❖

Perhaps the most frequently used technique for helping students construct initial models for procedural knowledge is think-aloud modeling. Although think-aloud modeling has been used for years to teach behavior modification strategies, Madeline Hunter (1976) has brought this technique to the attention of American educators (see Meichenbaum 1977 for a review of the use of think-aloud modeling). Think-aloud modeling involves the teacher expressing her thoughts and, thus, presenting a model for the procedure as she works through a skill or process. For example, if a teacher were to use think-aloud modeling to help students construct a model for the process of reading a bar graph, she might use an overhead of the graph and say to the class, "Let's see, what's the first thing I should do here? I'll read the title to get a sense of what this graph is all about. Then, I'll look at the horizontal axis—that's the line on the bottom." As the teacher thinks through the algorithm, tactic, or strategy, students get a glimpse of the steps or heuristics that are involved and the pattern of decisions that are made within the skill or process.

A flow chart is another, slightly more structured, method of model construction. Lewis and Green (1982) note that flow charts provide students with visual representations of algorithms, tactics, or strategies and greatly improve their ability to construct a model. Figure 3.7 shows a flow chart that might be presented to or constructed by students to help them build a model to develop a tactic for reading a bar graph.

Flow charts like the one in Figure 3.7 are meant to be nonrigorous and informal. Flow charting for the purpose of model building does not have to follow the strict conventions used in computer programming, where specific symbols (e.g., circles, triangles) have specific meanings. In fact, following these strict conventions would probably inhibit students' model building because they would have to try to remember all the rules and symbols every time they drew a flow chart.

Shaping Procedural Knowledge

The shaping process is probably the most important part of developing procedural expertise. In this phase, learners alter the initial model of the skill or process (which was either provided by the teacher or constructed by them). Researchers have found that during this stage systematic errors are commonly introduced into a skill or process. For instance, Brown and Burton (1978) observed a middle school student produce the following two errors:

500	312
−65	−243
565	149

FIGURE 3.7
Flow Chart for Reading a Bar Graph

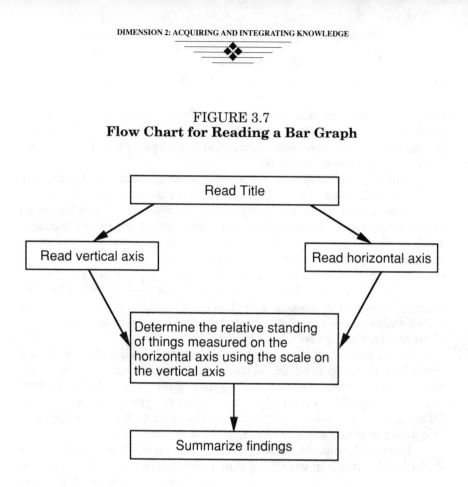

According to Anderson (1990), the response of most people (including some teachers) to such errors is to conclude that the student is extremely careless, is guessing randomly, or knows nothing. But this student was actually following faithfully a rule that he had constructed: $0 - N = N$; that is, "if a digit is subtracted from 0, the result is the digit." The infusion of systematic errors like this into an algorithm, a tactic, or a strategy is referred to as a "bug." Brown and Burton found 110 such bugs that young students may introduce into the subtraction process during the shaping phase of learning.

It is during the shaping phase, too, that learners attend to their conceptual understanding of a skill or process. When students lack conceptual understanding of skills and processes, they are liable to use procedures in shallow and ineffective ways. The Mathematical Science Education Board (1990) warns that procedural learning in itself does not ensure conceptual understanding. And Clement, Lockhead, and Mink (1979) have shown that even a solid knowledge of the steps involved in algebraic procedures does not in most cases (over 80 percent) imply an ability to correctly interpret the concepts underlying the procedures. Additionally, several studies have shown that mathematical procedures are best used when learned at a conceptual level (Davis 1984, Romberg and Carpenter 1986).

Guided practice is a powerful instructional technique for helping students understand procedural knowledge at a conceptual level. Although the term is most commonly associated with the work of Madeline Hunter, it has a rich tradition and theory base stemming from Vygotsky's work on the zone of proximal development and the more recent work on scaffolding. Vygotsky (1978) hypothesized that a learner needs the most guidance when working in the zone of development in which she has not yet acquired a skill but has some initial idea of it—in effect, when the learner is shaping a procedure she has been introduced to. What is now called scaffolded instruction is, at its core, guiding a learner through the shaping of a skill or process.

In guided practice, a teacher (or anyone else familiar with the procedure being learned) supervises the learner as she slowly moves through the process. The job of the expert guide is to help the learner experience possible pitfalls when performing the procedure. Recall Mrs. Baker's actions. She took great pains to illustrate a variety of errors that learners can make while performing three-column addition.

During the shaping process, it is also important to illustrate the different situations in which the skill or process can be used. To do this, Ms. Baker would have provided students with a variety of types of problems that require three-column addition. This is described as "developing the contextual knowledge important to a skill or procedure" (Paris and Lindauer 1982; Paris, Lipson, and Wixson 1983).

It's important to deal with only a few examples during the shaping phase of learning a new skill or process. The shaping phase is not the time to press students to perform a skill with any speed. Unfortunately, Healy (1990) reports that American educators tend to prematurely engage students in a heavy practice schedule and rush them through multiple examples. In contrast, Japanese educators attend to the needs of the shaping process by slowly walking through only a few examples:

> Whereas American second graders may spend thirty minutes on two or three pages of addition and subtraction equations, the Japanese are reported to be more likely at this level to use the same amount of time in examining two or three problems in depth, focusing on the reasoning process necessary to solve them (Healy 1990, p. 281).

In short, shaping through guided practice requires a knowledgeable teacher who slowly works with students at a conceptual level.

Internalizing Procedural Knowledge

The final stage of learning a skill or a process is to internalize the knowledge: to practice it to the point where you can perform it with relative ease. Actually, it is most accurate to think of skills and processes as being located on a continuum of skill levels ranging from controlled processing to automaticity (LaBerge and Samuels 1974, Shiffrin and Schneider 1977). Algorithms are commonly learned to the point of automaticity. For example, many algorithmic aspects of driving a car or comprehending language are learned at the automatic level. Controlled processes, on the other hand, require conscious thought even when perfected. For example, many of the strategies used in chess require conscious thought, even when used by experts. Internalizing, then, involves learning a procedure to the point at which it can be used with ease, whether it is performed automatically or with conscious control.

Regardless of whether a process is learned to the level of automaticity or the level of expert control, it is extended practice that gets the learner there. This was dramatically illustrated by Kollers (1976, 1979), who taught subjects to read passages that were inverted and backwards. After reading 200 pages, Kollers' subjects were able to read the inverted passages almost as quickly as they could read regular passages. As Anderson (1990) notes, such studies demonstrate that with enough practice, we can internalize skills and processes regardless of their nature. When skills are internalized, we don't have to pay attention to them and, thus, we can devote more attention to processing new information.

There does not seem to be any limit to the effects of practice, though after a certain amount of time the returns certainly diminish. Describing a study done on a woman who made her living rolling cigars in a cigar factory, Anderson notes:

> There do not appear to be any cognitive limits on the speed with which a skill can be performed. Her speed of cigar making . . . [improved] . . . over a period of ten years. When she finally stopped improving, it was discovered that she had reached the physical limit of the machinery with which she was working! (Anderson 1990, p. 261).

In short, it is practice—a lot of it—that enables the learner to internalize a skill or process.

Probably the most detailed work on practice as an instructional device has been done in the field of precision teaching, an instructional method developed by Ogden Lindsley (1972). The techniques of this method have been used in virtually every academic discipline, and a powerful organization headed by Carl Binder has sprung up to support it. Highly behavioristic in nature, precision teaching involves periodically measuring students' speed and accuracy in performing a skill and then marking each measurement on a "Standard Behavior Chart." Using the chart, students and teachers can observe progress until a specific goal is met.

Precision teaching is a time-consuming and rigorous way of internalizing a skill. Although very powerful, this method is probably far too labor-intensive for most teachers. Some aspects of precision teaching, however, can be readily adapted to classroom instruction—namely, practicing with specific goals of speed and accuracy in mind. For example, a teacher in San Diego who uses an adaptation of precision teaching explained to me how she emphasizes speed and accuracy when her students practice a new skill, such as dividing by fractions. To enhance accuracy, she periodically provides students with sample problems, which they perform independently in a set period of time. They then chart their accuracy. Over two weeks, students might do this four to seven times. Their chart provides a visual record of their progress. The same technique is used to enhance their speed.

Planning for the Acquisition and Integration of Procedural Knowledge

Instruction that will help students acquire and integrate procedural knowledge is usually the result of a teacher's careful planning. To illustrate, let's consider Ms. Conklin's planning for the weather unit.

Ms. Conklin's Planning for Dimension 2: Procedural Knowledge

As Ms. Conklin plans how she will help students acquire and integrate declarative knowledge, she also considers procedural knowledge. She starts by asking herself a basic question: "What skills and processes will students encounter in the unit?" She comes up with three ideas:

- Predict weather
- Read a barometer
- Operate the computer simulator at the university forecasting center

The more she thinks about it, though, the more she realizes that students don't need to know how to perform some of these processes; they simply need to be aware of them. For example, Ms. Conklin doesn't really expect students to be able to use the computer simulator with any level of expertise. She only wants students to have the experience of using a simulator. With this realization, she changes her question: "What skills and processes do students really need to master?" She decides there is only one: the process of reading a barometer, which students will be expected to be able to do later in science class.

Next, Ms. Conklin thinks about how she can help students develop a model for the process of reading a barometer. She decides that she will think aloud as she performs the process and write the steps on the blackboard as she does so. She will also ask students to create a flow chart of the process. She records her decisions in the planning guide (see column 2 of Figure 3.8 on page 64). To help students in the shaping process, she decides that she will ask a few students to read the barometer in front of the whole class. As they do so, she will ask "what if" questions that will make students aware of the errors they might easily make when reading a barometer. She realizes that she will have to practice reading a barometer herself to be able to identify and point out the pitfalls in the process. Finally, to help students develop their ability to a level of automaticity, she will establish a practice schedule for them and ask them to keep track of their accuracy. Again, she records her decisions in the planning guide.

Ms. Conklin's example illustrates four questions important to planning for procedural knowledge:

1. Which skills and processes do students really need to master? Many teachers fall into the trap of trying to help students master all the skills and processes presented in a unit. Students don't need to master everything. To decide which skills and processes to teach in the manner described in this chapter, the general rule of thumb is to select that those are necessary for students' present or future success. For example, the process of using a telescope might be covered in an introductory course on astronomy, even though it is not considered essential to successfully acquiring and integrating the important knowledge of the course. In this case, the teacher would probably simply demonstrate the process, so that students are aware of it, and ask them to try it a few times.

Some skills and processes, though important to present or future success in a content area, are familiar enough to students that extensive instruction isn't necessary. For example, if students are already quite

FIGURE 3.8
Unit Planning Guide for
Dimension 2: Acquiring and Integrating Procedural Knowledge

Skills/processes to be taught	How will students be aided in constructing models?	How will students be aided in shaping skills/processes?	How will students be aided in internalizing skills/processes?
Reading a barometer	• Think-aloud demonstration; write steps on the board. • Students will develop flow charts in cooperative groups.	• Demonstrate variations and errors • Have students work problems; ask "what if?" questions	• Time will be provided for students to practice in pairs—goal is 5 consecutive correct readings • Practice schedule will include spaced ½-hour sessions

proficient at reading a bar graph, they might easily internalize the process of reading another type of graph without going through the model building, shaping, and internalizing phases described here. Selecting the skills and processes that actually require attention to the three phases of learning procedural knowledge is a key curricular decision.

2. How will students be aided in constructing models? Given the importance of model building to procedural learning, teachers should be sure to attach some type of model-building instruction to important skills or processes in a unit. Ms. Conklin used think-aloud modeling, writing out the steps of the procedure, and flow charting. Such techniques help students establish the initial model. Without that model, procedural learning is reduced to trial and error.

3. How will students be aided in shaping the skill or process? Shaping is the most often overlooked part of learning procedural knowledge. Besides requiring an in-depth knowledge of the skill or process being taught, shaping demands time and energy, commodities that the typical school atmosphere works against. Successful shaping requires teachers to think about the various kinds of errors that can be made within the skill or process and the various contexts in which the skill or process might be used. In short, if teachers plan to help students shape a skill or process, they themselves need to have a high level of expertise in it. Recall that Ms. Conklin found that she had to practice reading a barometer herself before she could guide students through the shaping process.

4. How will students be aided in internalizing the skill or process? Key considerations here are how much and what kind of practice will be considered. Following the axiom of combined, massed, and distributed practice, a teacher might set up several practice sessions spaced fairly close together in the early stages of internalizing a skill or process. Over time, the practice sessions would be spaced further and further apart. The teacher must also decide what emphasis she will place on speed and accuracy during practice. In general, the more accuracy and speed with which a skill or procedure can be performed, the freer learners are to devote the limited capacity of short-term memory to dealing with other issues, thus increasing the flexibility of their performance.

❖ ❖ ❖

In summary, the acquisition and integration of declarative and procedural knowledge is basic to the learning process. Although somewhat similar, the two types of knowledge require different emphases. When acquiring and integrating declarative knowledge, the learner must initially construct meaning by associating new knowledge with prior knowledge. Then she must organize the information so as to emphasize important ideas and relationships. Finally, if she wants to retain the information in long-term memory, she must do something to help her store the information. When acquiring and integrating procedural knowledge, the learner must initially build a detailed model of the process involved. Then he must shape the process by eliminating errors and identifying the most efficient techniques for completing the process. Finally, he must practice the process until he can perform it with relative ease.

To help students acquire and integrate declarative and procedural knowledge, a teacher must have a keen understanding of both types of knowledge and be able to plan instruction that is sensitive to their differences.

4

❖

DIMENSION 3
Extending and Refining
Knowledge

❖

I f the purpose of learning were simply to acquire and integrate knowledge, little more would have to be done instructionally than has already been described in Dimensions 1 and 2. But learning is not a simple matter of being "filled up" with content and skills that rest neatly in niches in the mind. The most effective learning occurs when we continually cycle through information, challenging it, refining it. The content in any field should be thought of as "a landscape that is explored by criss-crossing it in many directions" (Spiro et al. 1987, p. 178). In more cognitive terms, once information is acquired and stored in long-term memory, it can be changed—and in the most effective learning situations, it is changed.

Many researchers attest to this dynamic aspect of human learning. For example, Piaget (1971) described two basic types of learning: one in which information is integrated into the learner's existing knowledge base, called *assimilation,* and another in which existing knowledge structures are changed, called *accommodation.* Other researchers and theorists have made similar distinctions. For example, Rumelhart and Norman (1981) described three basic types of learning. The first two, called *accretion* and *tuning,* deal with the gradual accumulation or addition of information over time and the expression of that information in more parsimonious ways. The third type of learning, called *restructuring,* involves reorganizing information so that it produces new insights and can be used in new situations.

It is the type of learning described by Piaget as accommodation and by Rumelhart and Norman as restructuring that interests us here. Dimension 3, extending and refining knowledge, is the aspect of learning that involves examining what is known at a deeper, more analytical level. Unfortunately, it is this aspect of learning that American students seem to neglect. The National Assessment of Educational Progress (NAEP), in a summary report of twenty years of findings from all the major content areas, notes that "on one hand, schools can be congratulated for increasing the percentages of students learning basic facts and procedures. However, while we have raised performance at the lower levels of the distribution, we have lost ground at the higher levels" (Mullis, Owen, and Phillips 1990, p. 36). A strong theme in the NAEP report is the need for American students to engage in more analytic activities that require a depth of reasoning about content—activities that extend and refine knowledge.

The number of activities that help extend and refine knowledge is probably infinite. But there is a finite set of activities that are particularly suited to content area instruction. These activities are comparison, classification, induction, deduction, error analysis, constructing support, abstracting, and analyzing perspective. Each of these is briefly described in Figure 4.1.

Each of the cognitive operations in Figure 4.1 is particularly suited to engaging learners in a way that allows learners to refashion their knowledge of content. In a social studies class, for example, students might compare democracy and dictatorship to discover new distinctions between them. In a science class, students might make deductions about whales based on known characteristics of mammals to refine and extend their knowledge about mammals and whales.

I should point out that the cognitive operations in Figure 4.1 may also be used when initially acquiring knowledge. For example, when first learning about types of governments, students may compare, induce, deduce, and so on, but they will probably do so automatically, without conscious thought. To extend and refine knowledge, students need to use these operations consciously and rigorously and in more complex ways. For example, when students first learn about democracies and republics, they might think casually about similarities and differences between the two. To extend and refine these concepts, however, they would be asked to list these similarities and differences, perhaps using some type of graphic representation or matrix. The difference is a matter of degree, focus, and conscious use.

The mental operations in Figure 4.1 can be used as activities for extending and refining knowledge in two basic ways, as illustrated by Mr. Walker's class and Ms. Hildebrandt's class.

FIGURE 4.1
Activities for Extending and Refining Knowledge

Comparing: Identifying and articulating similarities and differences between things.

Classifying: Grouping things into definable categories on the basis of their attributes.

Inducing: Inferring unknown generalizations or principles from observation or analysis.

Deducing: Inferring unstated consequences and conditions from given principles and generalizations.

Analyzing Errors: Identifying and articulating errors in your own or others' thinking.

Constructing Support: Constructing a system of support or proof for an assertion.

Abstracting: Identifying and articulating the underlying theme or general pattern of information.

Analyzing Perspectives: Identifying and articulating personal perspectives about issues.

Mr. Walker's Class

Mr. Walker is about to introduce the concept of individual retirement accounts (IRAs) in his business class. Although students have heard the term before and have some knowledge of IRAs, the section in the text they are about to read provides a detailed description of their characteristics. Mr. Walker starts the class by asking students what they already know about IRAs. He writes the term IRA on the blackboard and puts a circle around it. As students call out what they already know or think they know, Mr. Walker records the comments on the board as spokes emanating from a hub, the term IRA. The activity naturally leads to a discussion of IRAs and the notion of saving for the future. When Mr. Walker feels that students have had adequate time to construct meaning for the new concept, he asks them to read pages 95–97 of the text and answer the following questions:

- How is an IRA like a savings account and how is it different?
- Based on the information in the text, what generalizations can you make about IRAs?

At first students don't react strongly to the assignment. They think it's fairly simple. As they try to answer the questions, though, they discover they have to go well beyond the information presented in the text. For example, they realize they have to rethink what they know about savings accounts. But no matter where they look in their notes and the book, they cannot find a comparison of IRAs and saving accounts. Coming up with generalizations about IRAs is even more difficult. There is nothing in the text or in their notes that even hints at an answer. What looked like an easy assignment turns out to be challenging and time-consuming.

Ms. Hildebrandt's Class

Ms. Hildebrandt is in the middle of a unit on modern American artists. She has presented the works of fifteen different artists in two weeks. Students seem to be doing well. They can describe the characteristic techniques of each artist. They even remember something about the life of each artist. Ms. Hildebrandt decides to challenge students by giving them the following assignment:

> Classify the fifteen artists we have studied into at least three groups. When you're done, describe the defining characteristics of each group and explain why your categories are useful.

At first Ms. Hildebrandt gives her students two class periods to work on the assignment in groups of three. She soon finds that they need more time and more guidance. She has to take an entire class period just to teach students how to classify—how to develop rules to form categories and so on. She takes another full period to help students sort through all the different characteristics that might be used to form categories. What she thought would take two periods ends up taking five.

These classes illustrate two basic ways a teacher can use extending and refining activities in the classroom: (1) as a framework for questioning and (2) as directed activities. Mr. Walker used two of the eight extending and refining operations to construct questions. Although these questions were fairly easy to construct and were quickly presented to students, they still challenged students' understanding of the content.

In Ms. Hildebrandt's class, the extending and refining activity was much more structured and directed; the teacher presented criteria and directed classroom activity. In this chapter, we will consider both these methods of using extending and refining activities.

A Framework for Questioning

Teachers have long known and researchers have validated that questioning is an important way to cue students' use of specific thinking processes. As Cazden (1986) explains, the types of questions asked in the classroom develop the academic culture of the classroom. A great deal of evidence shows that open-ended essay questions require more analytic thinking than do closed yes/no questions or multiple-choice questions (Christenbury and Kelly 1983), but there has been considerable debate over what constitutes higher-level questions (Fairbrother 1975, Wood 1977). Whether the questions based on the eight extending and refining operations are on a "higher level" is a matter of academic debate and not of much concern in the Dimensions model. What is important is that the questions cue specific types of analytic thinking that have the power to change students' existing knowledge. Below are some sample questions for each of the eight extending and refining areas that teachers might use to elicit analytic thinking.

Comparison
 • How are these things alike? What particular characteristics are similar?
 • How are they different? What particular characteristics are different?

Classification
 • Into what groups could you organize these things?
 • What are the rules for membership in each group?
 • What are the defining characteristics of each group?

Induction
 • Based on the following facts (or observations), what can you conclude?
 • How likely is it that _____ will occur?

Deduction
 • Based on the following generalization (or rule or principle) what predictions can you make or what conclusions can you draw that must be true?

- If _____, then what can you conclude must happen?
- What are the conditions that make this conclusion inevitable?

Error Analysis
- What are the errors in reasoning in this information?
- How is this information misleading?
- How could it be corrected or improved?

Constructing Support
- What is an argument that would support the following claim?
- What are some of the limitations of or assumptions underlying this argument?

Abstracting
- What is the general pattern underlying this information?
- To what other situations does the general pattern apply?

Analyzing Perspectives
- Why would someone consider this to be good (or bad or neutral)?
- What is the reasoning behind their perspective?
- What is an alternative perspective and what is the reasoning behind it?

These questions and adaptations of them might be asked before, during, or after learning experiences. For example, before reading a chapter in a mathematics text, a teacher might ask students, "What statements about trapezoids must be true, based on the rules described in the chapter?" This question would stimulate deductive thinking about trapezoids. While students in a literature class are watching a film about Hemingway, a teacher might cue analysis through comparison by asking, "How does the information in this film about Hemingway's life compare with the information in the chapter you read?" After students have gone on a field trip as part of a business class, a teacher might ask, "Into what groups would you classify the seven business people we met? What are the distinguishing characteristics for each of your categories?"

An even more powerful use of extending and refining questions is to ask students to construct and answer their own. The teacher need only introduce students to the various types of questions and then invite them to devise their own questions. When I mention this alternative in workshops, teachers frequently respond that students would structure questions that are too easy. Although I have no research evidence to counter this assertion, I do have anecdotal evidence. A mathematics teacher in Michigan told me of her experience in asking students to create their own extending and refining questions during a unit on fractions. In previous units, she had introduced the eight types of extending and refining operations, and on a wall chart were listed questions like those above that related to each of the extending and refining areas. She made sure that students had adequate preparation for the assignment, which was simply to "write at least two questions about the chapter that cover at least two of the eight areas illustrated on the wall chart. Answer your questions in writing and hand in both your questions and your answers."

To the teacher's surprise, the questions students asked of themselves far surpassed the level of difficulty she thought them capable of handling. One student, for example, asked a deductive question that required him to infer characteristics about fractions based on axioms implicit in the chapter. Another student asked a classification question that required her to organize all the sample problems in the chapter into groups and describe the defining characteristics of each group. In short, this mathematics teacher found that the kinds of thinking that extend and refine knowledge *can* be elicited through questions constructed by students.

Directed Extending and Refining Activities

A teacher can also engage students in more elaborate extending and refining activities. Such activities are more detailed and generally require more time and resources than the activities associated with the types of questions described in the previous section. Directed extending and refining activities might be likened to what Stauffer (1970) calls directed reading/thinking activities: well-structured activities that elicit specific types of analytic thinking from students and guide them through the execution of that thinking. Let's look at the directed extending and refining activities that are included in Dimensions of Learning.

Comparison

Comparison is one of the most basic of all the extending and refining operations. In fact, it is so basic that some teachers believe it is not a high enough level of thinking to extend and refine students' knowledge. They reason that "all students can compare things without much trouble. How could it push their thinking in any way?" Of course, it is true that we quite naturally compare information, but recall that when we use comparison as an extending and refining activity, we use it consciously and rigorously. Unfortunately, American students, once again, do not perform well on this more rigorous type of comparison task.

In a summary report of twenty years of testing, NAEP commented on American students' ability to perform analytic comparison tasks:

> On an analytic task that asked students to compare food on the frontier (based on information presented) and today's food (based on their own knowledge), just 16 percent of the students at grade 8 and 27 percent at grade 12 provided an adequate or better response (Mullis et al. 1990, p. 16).

Stahl (1985) and Beyer (1988) have each developed comparison strategies that foster a high degree of analytic thinking. These strategies include the following basic steps:

- Specifying the items to be compared.
- Specifying the attributes or characteristics on which they are to be compared.
- Determining how they are alike and different.
- Stating similarities and differences as precisely as possible.

Creating directed comparison activities generally involves specifying certain aspects of the comparison process and asking students to generate the rest. For example, in a science class, a teacher might identify the processes of meiosis and mitosis. Students would then be asked to compare them using two or more important characteristics of their choice. It is identifying characteristics that are truly important that seems to be the critical feature of analytic comparison and the most difficult aspect of the task. For example, according to NAEP, when students were asked to provide a written response contrasting the key powers of the president of the United States today with those of George Washington, only 40 percent of the 12th graders could muster at least two important characteristics (Mullis et al. 1990, p. 24).

To be an effective analytic tool, then, comparison should focus students' attention on characteristics considered important to the items being compared. Teachers can foster students' ability to select important characteristics by initially using teacher-structured comparison tasks: tasks in which the teacher specifies both the elements to be compared and the characteristics on which they will be compared. Here is an example of a teacher-structured task:

> How do diamond and zirconium compare in terms of their scarcity? What would happen in the marketplace if one or the other should become more scarce? For the two characteristics identified above (their scarcity and the effects of their scarcity on the marketplace) describe how diamond and zirconium are similar and different.

❖

After assigning this task, the teacher and students would discuss why "scarcity" and the "effects of scarcity on the marketplace" are important characteristics in relation to diamond and zirconium. Once students were acquainted with the characteristics considered important to this topic, they would then be asked to engage in student-structured tasks. Here neither the elements to be compared nor the characteristics on which they are to be compared are specified:

> Select one naturally occurring and one man-made substance that might be usefully compared. Then select two or more characteristics on which to compare the two substances, such as problems that arise in production, differences in marketing and distribution, causes and effects of scarcity, and so on. Finally, describe how the substances are alike or different in terms of the characteristics you have selected.

Comparison, then, can be a powerful analytic tool when used rigorously to extend and refine knowledge.

Classification

Like comparison, classification is a type of thinking we engage in daily without much conscious thought. Mervis (1980) explains that we naturally categorize the world around us so we don't have to experience everything as new. Nickerson, Perkins, and Smith (1985) say that the ability to form conceptual categories is so basic to human cognition that it can be considered a necessary condition of thinking.

Although we use the process of classification quite naturally, when we use it to extend and refine our knowledge it can be very challenging. Beyer (1988) and others (Jones, Amiran, and Katims 1985; Taba 1967) have identified specific steps in the process of classification:

- Identifying the items to be classified.
- Initially sorting information into groups.
- Forming rules for categories and then reclassifying items based on these rules.

Constructing classification tasks to help students extend and re-fine their knowledge involves specifying certain aspects of the process and asking students to complete the others. For example, in a literature class a teacher might ask students to classify thirty characters from novels they have read. Students would initially sort the characters into rough groups. After this "first cut," there would invariably be some outliers or characters that do not fit into the initial categories. It is the existence of these outliers that makes the learner become more rigorous in defining categories. To place these outliers, students would have to redefine the categories and the rules for establishing the categories.

Classification as an analytic tool is powerful because it forces the learner to analyze semantic features to identify the salient features that determine membership in a group (Smith and Medin 1981). Making semantic feature analysis explicit in classification tasks is becoming increasingly popular, and a growing body of research indicates that classification emphasizing semantic feature analysis is a powerful tool for learning vocabulary (Pittleman, Heimlich, Berglund, and French 1991). Figure 4.2 shows the results of a semantic feature analysis task involving vocabulary words from a primary classroom.

Like comparison tasks, classification tasks might initially be structured by the teacher. Below is an example of a teacher-structured classification task that might be used in a geography class.

> There are many different regions in our state: neighborhoods, mountains, counties, cities, and so on. These regions can be organized into categories by considering how people use them. For example, people can use an area for dwellings, for recreation, or for natural resources; that is, we could classify the regions into three categories, based on their use: (1) those used for dwellings, (2) those used for recreation, and (3) those used for natural resources. In our state, examples of each of these categories of use exist. Provide at least three examples in our state for each of the three categories. Make sure you describe the defining characteristics of each category; for example, describe the characteristics of regions that are used for dwellings.

After discussing the features important to categories in a given content area, the teacher can assign other classification tasks that require students to create their own categories and identify the elements to be sorted into those categories:

> Regional categories can be made up of almost anything, depending on the elements you use to create them—people, land, automotive supply stores. Your task is to create categories by selecting a variety of elements that will allow you to distinguish one category from another. For example, you could decide that the presence of one school, one church, a gas station, and a convenience store signifies "a loose social neighborhood." Likewise, you could decide that an area with a ratio of three gas stations to one school may qualify as a business neighborhood, and a region of inverse ratio (three schools to one gas station) could be described as a "residential neighborhood." Make sure you have enough combinations to form at least five categories. Finally, select an area within the greater metropolitan area and identify at least one example of each category you have

FIGURE 4.2
Semantic Feature Analysis Task

Classroom SFA Grid for Vehicles

Vehicles	two wheels	four wheels	more than four wheels	motor	diesel fuel	gasoline	people power	handlebars	passengers	enclosed	used on land	used on water
car	−	+	−	+	+	−	−	+	+	+	−	
bicycle	+	−	−	−	−	+	+	−	−	+	−	
motorcycle	+	−	−	+	+	−	+	+	−	+	−	
truck	−	−	+	+	+	−	−	+	+	+	−	
train	−	−	+	+	−	−	−	+	+	+	−	
skateboard	−	+	−	−	−	+	−	−	−	+	−	
rowboat	−	−	−	−	−	+	−	+	−	−	+	
sailboat	−	−	−	−	−	−	−	+	−	−	+	
motorboat	−	−	−	+	+	−	−	+	−	−	+	

Source: Pittelman, Heimlich, Berglund, and French 1991.
Copyright© 1991 by the International Reading
Association. Reprinted by permission.

established. Also explain why your categories are useful ways of thinking about regions.

Induction

Induction is probably the most basic of all higher-order cognitive operations. We make inductions anytime we draw conclusions based on evidence. For example, a student makes an induction when he concludes that the teacher is in a bad mood because she slammed her books down on the desk after she briskly walked into the room. Although induction is not treated overtly in all thinking skills programs, it is implicit in all.

Teachers can easily help students practice induction in the classroom, for the core of induction as an extending and refining activity is generating and verifying hypotheses. One teacher described to me how at the start of the Persian Gulf War, she asked students to generate hypotheses about Saddam Hussein's reasons for invading Kuwait. The students listed their hypotheses and the information supporting their hypotheses. As the war progressed, students gathered information that confirmed or disconfirmed their hypotheses. Over time, students changed and adapted their hypotheses. Although the students as a group did not reach a consensus, all the students experienced the inexact cycle of generating hypotheses, gathering data, reformatting hypotheses, and so on.

A powerful tool for fostering induction in the classroom is the "induction matrix" developed by Beau Fly Jones and her colleagues (personal communication 1987). Figure 4.3 shows an example of an induction matrix. Content area concepts (e.g., "democracy") head each row of the matrix, and questions to be answered about each concept (e.g., "Who governs?") head each column. Students first fill in the cells corresponding to each concept and each question, which in Figure 4.3 would be information about "who governs" in democracies, in republics, in monarchies, and so on. After they have filled in each of the basic cells, students make row and column inductions. Row inductions would be about democracies, republics, and so on. Column inductions would be about various types of governance, decision making, and so on. Finally, students make a "grand induction" and record it in the bottom right cell.

At a more sophisticated level of analysis, students might be asked to make inductions about the intentions behind materials they are reading. Cooper (1984) has identified four basic categories of intentions behind the use of language in oral or written form:

• *Constatives:* expressions of beliefs along with expressions of an intention that the audience form like beliefs.

FIGURE 4.3
Induction Matrix

	Who Governs	How Decisions Are Made	Earliest Examples	Conclusions
Democracy				
Republic				
Monarchy				
Dictatorship				
Conclusions				

• *Directives:* expressions of an attitude toward some prospective action by the audience along with an intention that the attitude be taken as a reason to act.

• *Commissives:* expressions of intentions to act along with expressions of belief that such expressions of intentions obligate one to act.

• *Acknowledgements:* expressions of feelings toward the audience.

Each of these categories of intentions has subcategories of intentions. These are listed in Figure 4.4 on page 80.

Once students are aware of the various types of intentions, they can induce these intentions from information they read or hear. As students soon discover, inducing authors' intentions is an inexact process of identifying the driving force behind the form and content of a text. It involves analyzing why specific words were selected, why certain rhetorical devices were used, and so on. To illustrate, as a result of analyzing the Declaration of Independence, one group of 12th graders induced that

FIGURE 4.4
Categories and Subcategories of Intentions

Constatives:

You *assert* if you express a proposition.

You *predict* if you express a proposition about the future.

You *recount* if you express a proposition about the past.

You *describe* if you express that someone or something consists of certain features.

You *ascribe* if you express that a feature applies to someone or something.

You *inform* if you express a proposition that your audience does not yet believe.

You *confirm* if you express a proposition along with support for it.

You *concede* if you express a proposition contrary to what you would like to or previously did believe.

You *retract* if you express that you no longer believe a proposition.

You *assent* if you express belief in a proposition already under discussion.

You *dissent* if you express disbelief in a proposition already under discussion.

You *dispute* if you express reason(s) not to believe a proposition already under discussion.

You *respond* if you express a proposition that has been inquired about.

You *suggest* if you express some, but insufficient, reason(s) to believe a proposition.

You *suppose* if you express that it is worth considering the consequences of a proposition.

Directives:

You *request* if you express that you desire your audience to act.

You *ask* if you express that you desire to know whether or not a proposition is true.

You *command* if you express that your authority is reason for your audience to act.

You *forbid* if you express that your authority is reason for your audience to refrain from acting.

You *permit* if you express that your audience's action is possible by virtue of your authority.

You *recommend* if you express the belief that there is good reason for your audience to act.

Commissives:

You *promise* if you express that you intend to act.

You *offer* if you express that you intend to act if and when your audience desires it.

Acknowledgments:

Apologies
Condolences
Congratulations
Greetings
Thanks

Source: Cooper 1984. Copyright© 1984 by the Guilford Press. Reprinted by permission.

one major intention of its authors was to *ascribe* specific highly negative characteristics to the reigning monarch of England. They cited as evidence for their induction the repeated use of a syntactic pattern beginning in the third paragraph of the Declaration:

> He has refused his Assent to Laws. . . .
>
> He has forbidden his Governors to pass Laws. . . .
>
> He has refused to pass other Laws. . . .
>
> He has. . . .
>
> He has. . . .

This "he has" pattern comprises thirteen consecutive one-sentence paragraphs and five additional paragraphs that together give the reader a strong impression of an unfair and uncompromising leader.

Students also found evidence that the authors of the Declaration were trying to *permit* their readers to act in ways counter to their natural inclination to submit to rule from England. According to Cooper (1984), the intention of permitting is a form of directive. Students believed the first paragraph of the Declaration was intended to establish a tone of permission by suggesting that the forthcoming Declaration was a necessary occurrence in the events of human history:

> When in the course of human events, it becomes necessary for one people to dissolve the political bands which have connected them with one another, and to assume among the powers of the earth, the separate and equal station to which the Laws of Nature and of Nature's God entitle them, a decent respect to the opinions of mankind requires that they should declare the causes which impel them to the separation.

Finally, some students found evidence for the commissive intention of a *promise*. They perceived the last paragraph of the Declaration to be a promise to do whatever was necessary to effect the establishment of a free and independent United States of America. This promise was particularly evident in the closing line: " . . . we mutually pledge to each other our Lives, our Fortunes, and our Sacred Honor."

Deduction

There is a fair amount of confusion about the distinction between induction and deduction. Anderson (1990) clarifies the distinction with the following illustration.

> The Abkhasian Republic of the USSR [in Georgia] has 10 men over 160. No other place in the world has a man over 160.

1. The oldest man in the world today is in the USSR.
2. The oldest man in the world tomorrow will be in the USSR.

He explains:

Conclusion *1* is deductively valid. If the premises are true, . . . then the conclusion must be true. However, conclusion *2* is only inductively valid, that is, it is a highly likely conclusion if the premises are true, but it is conceivable that all 10 men could die before tomorrow (Anderson 1990, p. 303).

As Anderson's example illustrates, deductive conclusions, given the validity of their premises, are absolute. Inductive conclusions, on the other hand, may be highly probable but they are never absolute. A common misconception is that deductive conclusions are used in mathematics but not in the humanities or social sciences. At a formal level, there is some truth to this, for mathematics is based on the use of axioms and theorems to generate deductive conclusions. In fact, one of the purest deductive activities is a mathematical proof (e.g., proving the validity of the Pythagorean theorem). Deductive reasoning is indigenous to mathematics, but why would anyone want to reinforce its use in other disciplines? First and foremost, much of our thinking, academic or otherwise, is deductive, though not consciously so. For instance, if someone says President Bush is going to veto the environmental bill because he's following standard Republican lines, that person would be reasoning deductively. His thought process breaks down to:

- All Republican presidents vote against environmental bills.
- George Bush is a Republican president.
- Therefore he will vote against the environmental bill.

As we shall see, reorganizing the implicit deductive conclusions in a content area can be a very powerful tool in extending and refining content knowledge.

Another, albeit less important, reason for fostering deductive reasoning in the classroom is that many of the tests we call "reasoning tests" are highly deductive in nature. Take, for example, the New Jersey Test of Reasoning Skills (Shipman 1983), which is administered across the United States as a measure of general reasoning ability. The three items below are patterned after the items in that test. Take a moment to answer them.

Item 1

Martha said, "Rectangles always have four corners. Joe said, "That's no different from saying that all rectangles are four-cornered things.

a. Joe is wrong. Martha is saying that all four-cornered things are rectangles.
b. Joe is right.
c. Joe is wrong. Martha is saying that some four-cornered things are rectangles.

Item 2

The City Water Department says, "If the water has been treated, it is safe to drink." Since the water in our town has been found to be unsafe to drink, it follows that:

a. The water was treated.
b. The water was not treated.
c. The treatment made the water unsafe.

Item 3

Jack is older than Bill. Herb is also older than Bill. Therefore, it follows that:

a. You can't tell who is oldest.
b. Jack and Herb are both the same age.
c. You can't tell who is the youngest.

Would you expect to find these questions on a junior high school test? If not, you're in good company. I recently administered the New Jersey Test of Reasoning Skills to thirty adults, all of whom had advanced degrees in education. Although they did not do poorly on the test, more than 80 percent felt "unsure" of their answers because they weren't "used to the type of thinking involved." After administering the test, I analyzed the fifty items on the test and found that 84 percent were deductive in nature. The unease these educated people felt probably stemmed from their unfamiliarity with the rather formal type of deductive arguments used in the test. It has become my strong bias that if we, as educators, are going to use highly deductive tests to measure general reasoning ability, then we are duty bound to provide students with some practice in the types of reasoning they include.

Most textbooks on deductive reasoning (e.g., Klenk 1983) identify three basic types of deductive arguments: categorical, conditional, and linear. Items 1, 2, and 3 above represent respectively these three types. Categorical arguments are by far the arguments most commonly found in tests of reasoning that include deductive reasoning. Of the fifty items on the New Jersey Test of Reasoning that I administered, for instance, twenty-four (or 48 percent) involved categorical arguments.

Although there are many formal rules for properly using categorical arguments, the basic steps for using them as activities to extend and refine knowledge are quite simple. Categorical arguments are composed of two premises and a conclusion that stems from the premises. The syllogism is the typical form of a categorical argument:

- All A are B.
- All B are C.
- Therefore all A are C.

The appearance of B in both premises enables a deductive conclusion to be drawn because B relates the information in the two premises. One of the first steps in using categorical arguments to extend and refine knowledge is to recognize what I call "hidden syllogisms" and state them in formal syllogistic form. This process is called *standardization* in the Philosophy for Children program (Lipman, Sharp, and Oscanyan 1980). Let's take the statement about George Bush and reword it into a more clearly syllogistic form:

Premise #1: All *Republican presidents* (A) are *people who vote against environmental issues* (B).

Premise #2: *George Bush* (C) is a *Republican president* (A).

Conclusion: Therefore, *George Bush* (C) is a *person who votes against environmental issues* (B).

It is the middle term, A, that appears in both premises and allows for a deduction to be made linking the term B with C.

Once students are aware of the form of categorical syllogisms and can standardize, or reword, statements so they reflect this syllogistic form, they can be asked to find syllogistic arguments in academic content. A junior high history teacher who had taught syllogisms to her students described to me what happened when she asked her students to analyze the Declaration of Independence for hidden syllogistic arguments. One group of students asserted that the logic underlying the Declaration could be stated in the following way:

Premise #1: Governments that should be supported and, consequently, not overthrown (A), protect the God-given rights of their people to life, liberty, and the pursuit of happiness. (B)

Premise #2: The Government of the present king of England (C) does not protect the God-given rights of the people to life, liberty, and the pursuit of happiness (B).

Conclusion: Therefore, the Government of the present king of
England (C) is not one that should be supported and,
consequently, not overthrown (A).

Stated in more abstract form, this syllogism might be written as
follows:

- All A are B.
- C is not B.
- Therefore C is not A.

All conclusions in syllogistic arguments are not valid. Once an
argument has been stated in syllogistic form, its validity can be analyzed, though. A useful tool in helping students determine the validity
of a syllogistic argument is the Euler diagram, named after Leonhard
Euler, the 18th century mathematician who used this kind of diagram
to teach logic to a German princess. The technique was, in fact, invented
by Leibniz and is often confused with the quite different method of Venn
diagrams (Johnson-Laird 1983). Euler diagrams use circles to represent
set membership. We might use the following Euler diagram to represent
the syllogism students found in the Declaration of Independence:

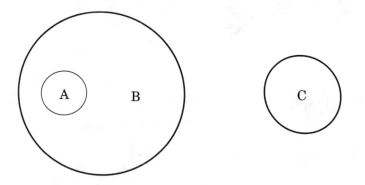

Looking at this diagram, we can clearly see that set C (the present
government of England) is not related to set A (governments that should
be supported and, consequently, not overthrown). After using the Euler
diagram, the junior high students concluded that the logic of the forgers
of the Declaration was sound. But more important, they applied critical
analysis to the reasoning behind a living document—a task that relatively few people have the tools to accomplish.

Recognizing and standardizing categorical syllogisms typically
uncovers errors in logic. For example, I recently heard a television
newscaster interview an individual who said, "Saddam Hussein is a
dictator because he tortures people, and we know that all dictators are

torturers." Standardized, the logic behind this statement might be written like this:

- Premise #1: All dictators (A) are people who torture (B).
- Premise #2: Saddam Hussein (C) is a person who tortures (B).
- Conclusion: Therefore, Saddam Hussein (C) is a dictator (A).

Although there is certainly a great deal of evidence that Saddam Hussein is a dictator, this deductive argument does not prove it, as we can see by constructing Euler diagrams. We can represent the first premise with this diagram:

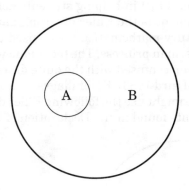

When you add the second premise, you can conclude only that C is a subset of B. C might not be related to A at all.

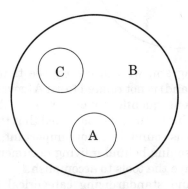

In fact, from the two premises given, we can draw no valid conclusion about the relationship between A and C.

The types of valid conclusions that can be drawn from syllogistic arguments are listed in Figure 4.5. What is perhaps most interesting about Figure 4.5 is that it reveals that only twenty-seven of the sixty-four possible forms of syllogistic arguments have valid conclusions.

Another way students can use syllogisms to extend and refine their knowledge is to analyze their truth. Copi (1972) explains that the *validity* of a syllogism depends on whether the conclusion follows from the premises. As Figure 4.5 illustrates, 42 percent of all the possible forms of syllogistic arguments have valid conclusions. A syllogism that has a valid conclusion still may not be true, though, because *truth* depends on the accuracy of the premises. Take, for example, the earlier syllogism involving President Bush. The conclusion (President Bush is a person who votes against environmental issues) is logically valid, but the entire syllogism is not true because of the inaccuracy of the first premise (All Republican presidents are people who vote against environmental issues). Analyzing the truth of syllogisms represents an entirely different type of analytic thinking that in the Dimensions of Learning model is called *error analysis.*

Error Analysis

No matter how intelligent or educated we are, we make errors. Thomas Gilovich (1991) identifies numerous examples of erroneous conclusions in everyday reasoning, some of them drawn by otherwise academically rigorous thinkers. Francis Bacon, for example, believed that warts could be cured by rubbing them with pork. Aristotle thought that male babies were conceived in a strong north wind. Other reports of the types of errors reasonable people make in everyday situations have been compiled by Johnson-Laird (1985) and by Perkins, Allen, and Hafner (1983). As Gilovich notes, studying the types of errors we make enlightens us not only about our thinking, but also about the subject in which we make the errors. In keeping with this premise, the California State Department of Education uses error analysis as a testing and teaching tool. Figure 4.6 on page 90 is an example of one of the open-ended questions it administers to students as a strategy for enhancing mathematical competence.

One of the most common types of errors made every day falls under the category of confirmatory bias, which is the tendency to seek out information that confirms our hypotheses. As Gilovich (1991) puts it:

> When trying to assess whether a belief is valid, people tend to seek out information that would confirm the belief over information that might disconfirm it. In other words, people ask questions or seek information for which the equivalent of a "yes" response would lend credence to their hypothesis (p. 33).

FIGURE 4.5
Valid Conclusions from Syllogistic Arguments

Second Premise	First Premise			
	All A are B	Some A are B	No A are B	Some A are not B
All B are C	All A are C	Some A are C / Some C are A	Some C are not A	
Some B are C			Some C are not A	
No B are C	No A are C / No C are A	Some A are not C		
Some B are not C				
All C are B			No A are C / No C are A	Some A are not C
Some C are B			Some C are not A	
No C are B	No C are A / No A are C			
Some C are not B	Some C are not A			

(continued)

FIGURE 4.5 (continued)

Second Premise	First Premise			
	All B are A	Some B are A	No B are A	Some B are not A
All B are C	Some A are C Some C are A	Some A are C Some C are A	Some C are not A	Some C are not A
Some B are C	Some A are C Some C are A		Some C are not A	
No B are C	Some A are not C	Some A are not C		
Some B are not C	Some A are not C			
All C are B	All C are A		No C are A No A are C	
Some C are B	Some C are A Some A are C		Some C are not A	
No C are B	Some A are not C	Some A are not C		
Some C are not B				

FIGURE 4.6

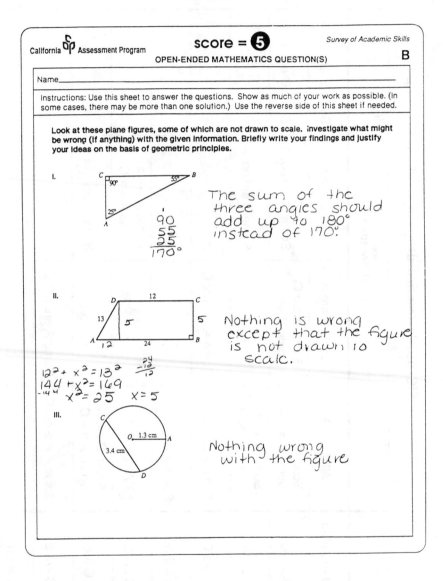

Wason and Johnson-Laird (1972) conducted a study in which subjects were given the following rule: "If a card has a vowel, then it has an even number on the other side." The subjects were then given cards like these:

The subjects were asked to turn over only those cards that had to be turned over to see if the rule was correct. Forty-six percent elected to turn over both the E and the 4. The E had to be turned over but the 4 did not. Only 4 percent elected to turn over the E and the 7, which is the correct choice of cards, since an odd number behind the E or a vowel behind the 7 would have broken the rule. Gilovich (1991) explains that the tendency for the subject not to turn over the 7 exemplifies the confirmative bias: we shy away from information that would prove a hypothesis false.

One of the most powerful ways I have seen this demonstrated in a classroom setting involved a teacher asking students to develop an argument against some strongly held belief. The teacher told me that she asked students to identify their position on the ban of fur sales and then work in cooperative groups to develop a strong argument supporting the position opposing their own. When the task was completed, few students had changed their opinion, but virtually all had identified the erroneous assumptions from which they had been operating. In fact, the culminating activity requested by students was to list all the incorrect assumptions and beliefs they discovered about their own thinking on the topic.

Informal fallacies are another type of error common in everyday reasoning, particularly when that reasoning is intended to "persuade." Lockwood and Harris (1985) assert that it is especially important to study these types of errors in a free society such as ours because much of the information we must process is persuasive in nature: someone is continually trying to get our vote, our money, or our agreement.

There are many descriptions of the kinds of informal fallacies that can be made in persuasive discourse, including those by Perkins, Allen, and Hafner (1983) and Toulmin (Toulmin 1958; Toulmin, Rieke, and Janik 1981). In the Dimensions of Learning model, informal fallacies are organized in three basic categories that are briefly described in Figure 4.7.

FIGURE 4.7
Informal Fallacies

Category I: Errors based on faulty logic
Errors that fall into this category use a type of reasoning that is flawed in some way or is simply not rigorous. Such errors include:

a. *Contradiction:* Someone presents information that is in direct opposition to other information within the same argument.
b. *Accident:* Someone fails to recognize that an argument is based on an exception to a rule.
c. *False cause:* Someone confuses a temporal order of events with causality, or someone oversimplifies a complex causal network.
d. *Begging the question (circularity):* Someone makes a claim and then argues for it by advancing grounds whose meaning is simply equivalent to that of the original claim.
e. *Evading the issue:* Someone sidesteps an issue by changing the topic.
f. *Arguing from ignorance:* Someone argues that a claim is justified simply because its opposite cannot be proved.
g. *Composition and division:* Composition involves someone asserting about a whole something that is true of its parts. Division involves someone asserting about all of the parts something that is true about the whole.

Category II: Errors based on attack
Informal fallacies in this category all use the strategy of attacking a person or position.

h. *Poisoning the well:* Someone is committed to his position to such a degree that he explains away absolutely everything others offer in opposition to his position.
i. *Arguing against the person:* Someone rejects a claim on the basis of derogatory facts (real or alleged) about the person making the claim.
j. *Appealing to force:* Someone uses threats to establish the validity of a claim.

Category III: Errors based on weak references
Informal fallacies that fall into this category appeal to something other than reason to make their point; however, they are not based on attack.

k. *Appealing to authority:* Someone evokes authority as the last word on an issue.
l. *Appealing to the people:* Someone attempts to justify a claim on the basis of popularity.
m. *Appealing to emotion:* Someone uses an emotion-laden or "sob" story as proof for a claim.

After introducing students to a small subset of these fallacies, a teacher might ask students to look for them in persuasive information they encounter. One of my favorite examples of the use of informal fallacies in the classroom comes from a literature teacher. After presenting these fallacies to students before the presidential election in 1988, the teacher asked students to observe the debate between candidates George Bush and Michael Dukakis. Their task was to identify the informal fallacies used by each candidate. To their chagrin, many students found their favorite candidate frequently made recognizable errors. Their knowledge of informal fallacies affected the way students processed information as the campaign progressed. They were less likely to accept the opinion of their favorite candidate without question and delved more deeply into issues.

Constructing Support

The other side of analyzing a persuasive argument for errors is constructing a sound argument. Of course, one aspect of creating a sound persuasive argument is avoiding the errors described above, but persuasion also involves using certain conventions. The art of persuasion has its roots in classical rhetoric, which is built on four basic devices, commonly called the "four appeals" (Kinneavy 1991):

1. Appealing to an audience through personality.
2. Appealing through accepted beliefs and traditions.
3. Appealing through rhetorical style.
4. Appealing through the logic of one's argument.

When the appeal is through personality, the speaker or writer tries to get the audience to like him. The information presented is usually about the speaker or writer—anecdotes about his life intended to make you, the audience, identify with him. The speaker or writer also frequently compliments the audience in an attempt to be perceived as a friend or an ally.

When the appeal is through beliefs and tradition, the writer or speaker often refers to allegedly accepted principles based on tradition. For example, the writer or speaker may assert that the principles underlying his argument "have always been held as true." He is using beliefs and tradition to evoke the power of culture, the power of "the way things are done around here."

Appeal through rhetorical style aims to persuade through the beauty of language, including how ideas are phrased, the intonation used in their presentation, and the physical gestures that accompany them. Goldman, Berquist, and Coleman (1989) describe in detail the elaborate systems that have been created throughout the centuries to improve the persuasive power of appeal through rhetorical style.

The last of the four appeals is logic. Students of rhetoric used to be taught the formal rules of syllogistic reasoning to improve their ability to appeal through logic. In recent years, less formal and more flexible systems have been developed. The most common is that developed by Toulmin (Toulmin, Rieke, and Janik 1981). Although Toulmin's system has multiple aspects, his basic structure of an argument based on reason has four simple components:

- *Evidence.* Information that leads to a claim. For example: Last night five crimes were committed within two blocks of one another.
- *Claim.* The assertion that something is true: The crime rate in our city is escalating dramatically.
- *Elaboration.* Examples of or explanations for the claim: The dramatic increase can be seen by examining the crime rates in the downtown area over the last twenty years.
- *Qualifier.* A restriction on the claim or evidence counter to the claim: The crime rate has stabilized in some areas, however.

Once students understand the four types of appeals, they can analyze persuasive arguments. For example, a social studies teacher told me that he regularly asks students to analyze information from television, textbooks, and newspapers to determine which of the four types of appeals is being used. He attested to students' ability to perform such analyses with accuracy and enthusiasm.

Abstracting

The term abstracting is used frequently in conversations about learning and thinking. Webster's New Collegiate Dictionary says that to "abstract" is to remove, to separate, "to consider apart from application to or association with a particular instance." You would be abstracting if you looked at one situation and identified basic elements of the situation that occur in another situation. For instance, let's look at the situation below:

> When C. L. Holes was inventing a typewriting machine in the early 1870s, he found that the machine jammed if he typed too fast. So he deliberately arranged the positions of the letters in a way that forced typists to work slowly. Nevertheless, Sholes' typewriter design was still a great improvement over earlier models, and it was soon in use all over the world.
>
> Today, even though typewriters have been improved in many ways, nearly all of them have keyboards like the one Sholes devised

in 1872. The letter arrangement is called QWERT, after the five left-hand keys in the top letter row. You can see QWERT keyboards on computer consoles as well as on typewriters. Unfortunately, the QWERT arrangement slows typing, encourages errors, and causes greater fatigue than another arrangement devised by August Dvorak in 1930, which has proved in several tests to be much faster and more accurate than QWERT.

Millions of people have learned the QWERT keyboard, however, and it is being taught to students in schools right now. So it seems that we will continue to live with this 19th century mistake.

Now think about how you might abstract this situation. You might first liken the history of the QWERT keyboard to that of the measuring system used in the United States. When asked to describe how they are alike, you would probably explain the connection in the following way: "In both situations, something was created that was initially very useful (QWERT and the British system of measurement). Then something better came along (the Dvorak system and the metric system), but the new invention was not used because everyone was so familiar with the old invention."

The psychological phenomenon that allows you to make the connection between the two seemingly unrelated events is the identification of a "general" or "abstract" pattern of information that applies to both situations. Here is the general pattern for the above example:

- Something useful is created.
- Something better comes along.
- It is rejected because people resist change.

It is the identification of a general pattern that is central to the abstracting process. From this perspective, we might say that the process of abstracting is at the heart of metaphor. Ortony (1989) explains that a metaphor contains two basic components, a topic and a vehicle. The topic is the principal subject to which the vehicle (the metaphoric term) is applied. If we say that A is a B when A is not actually a B, then A would be the topic and B would be the vehicle. Consider the metaphor "Love is a rose." Here, love is the topic and rose is the vehicle. Love is not related to rose at a literal level but it is related at an abstract level, as shown in Figure 4.8. Speaking of the importance of metaphor, Ortony notes:

> It is more than a linguistic or psychological curiosity. It is more than rhetorical flourish. It is also a means of conveying and acquiring new knowledge and of seeing things in new ways. It may well be that metaphors are closely related to insight (Ortony 1980, p. 361).

FIGURE 4.8
Abstractions in a Metaphor

Literal Attributes of Love	Shared Abstract Attributes	Literal Attributes of Rose
an emotion		a flower
sometimes pleasant	desirable	beautiful
can be associated with unpleasant experiences	double-edged	has thorns
often occurs in adolescence		comes in different colors

Teachers can use abstracting in the classroom in several ways. Comparing literary works is particularly suited to analysis by abstraction. After students have read a selection, they can be asked to identify the underlying abstract pattern of the content. For example, after reading *The Old Man and the Sea* students might first identify the key points of the novel:

- The old man and boy had a close relationship.
- The old man had a spell of bad luck in his fishing.
- The boy had faith in the old man.
- The old man hooked a large fish, and so on.

Once the key points or literal pattern of the novel are established, students then transform the ideas into a more abstract or general pattern:

Key Points		Abstract Pattern
Old man and boy had a close relationship.	→	Two people have a close relationship.
Old man had a spell of bad luck.	→	One of the partners experiences difficulties.
The young boy had faith in the old man.	→	The other partner is highly supportive.
The old man hooked a large fish.	→	The partner experiencing difficulty is faced with a difficult challenge that can bring him success.
The old man did not land the fish intact, but still resolved a basic conflict in his life.	→	The partner does not directly meet the challenge but still works out some basic issues in his life.

The abstract form identified, students then look for another piece of literature or another situation to which the abstract form applies. For example, using the abstracting process with *The Lord of the Flies*, one student described how the same abstract pattern in Golding's work also applied to a story she had seen on television about the birth of a street gang in east Los Angeles. Another student saw the abstract pattern in *The Lord of the Flies* applying to Mussolini's rise to power in pre–World War II Italy.

The abstracting process is well suited to many content areas. Here is an abstracting task that teachers might present to students in a history class:

Identify the generic elements or basic elements of the war in Vietnam. Then identify another situation that has nothing to do with wars between nations and describe how that situation fits the basic elements you have identified.

I have seen abstraction used by a science teacher who asked students to relate the functioning of a cell to the workings of a city and by a mathematics teacher who asked students to relate basic mathematical operations to relationships in nature.

Analyzing Perspectives

The final type of extending and refining activity in the Dimensions of Learning model is analyzing perspectives. Analyzing perspectives involves identifying your position or stance on an issue and the reasoning behind that stance. It also involves considering a perspective different from your own. Your perspective on an issue is usually related to some underlying value you hold. Value and affect are functionally related: you have a certain emotional response to a situation because you interpret your experiences partly through your values. For example, if you respond with anger to the treatment of Boo in *To Kill A Mockingbird*, it is because one of your underlying values is that human beings should be respected regardless of their intellectual capabilities. Paul (1984, 1987) has noted that, given the complexity of our society, the ability to recognize our values and the reasons behind them and to acknowledge another system of reasoning that would yield a different value is one of the most important intellectual skills a person can develop. Fisher and Ury (1981) assert that this skill is at the heart of negotiation.

To practice the process of analyzing perspectives, students can systematically analyze their values as they are triggered by learning experiences; ultimately, this process will help them understand (though not necessarily agree with) other systems of values. At a basic level, the process involves:

• Acknowledging your emotional responses.
• Identifying the specific concept or statement that has triggered the responses.
• Describing the specific value represented by the concept or statement.
• Describing the reasoning or belief systems behind the value.
• Articulating an opposing value.
• Describing the reasoning behind that value.

This process is most commonly used in the context of an argument or conflict. For example, in a conversation about abortion, Person A might assert that abortion should be banned. In response, Person B might become angry. If person B were to stop and analyze perspectives, she would first acknowledge her strong emotional response (anger), and the specific concept or statement that triggered it (abortion should be banned). Then she would try to determine the underlying value represented by that statement, which in this case might be the idea that life should never be taken by another human being. At a much higher analytical level, she would try to discern the system of reasoning or beliefs underlying the value. Because systems of beliefs are invariably the foundation of values, identifying them is the very core of analyzing perspectives. In this case, Person B might discover that Person A's belief that life begins at conception is the underlying principle driving her value and consequent reaction to abortion. Person B would then articulate a value counter to this (abortion should not be banned) and a system of reasoning or beliefs that would logically support the value (life does not begin at conception).

This is an oversimplified example of a process that Paul (1984, 1987) and others assert has the power to create great personal insight and flexibility in dealing with others. As a tool for extending and refining knowledge it has wide application. For example, students might use the process with essays on the ethics of the U.S. invasion of Iraq in 1991. The teacher would present students with an editorial strongly in favor of (or against) the U.S. invasion of Iraq. Students would then try to identify their reaction to the editorial, the specific concept or statement they have reacted to, the value underlying their reaction, and the system of beliefs underlying that value. Students who have similar reactions might form a cooperative group. The group would then articulate an opposing value and a possible system of beliefs underlying it. Cooperative groups could present their findings orally or in writing, along with statements of the personal awareness the process created.

Teaching the Extending and Refining Processes

As you no doubt inferred from the previous discussion, the extending and refining operations can be rather complex processes that include steps or general rules. In short, they themselves are types of procedural knowledge. Within the thinking skills movement, there is some debate about whether these mental processes should be taught directly to students. On one side of the issue are theorists such as Beyer (1988), who assert that students need direct instruction and practice in these mental processes in a content-free environment. At the other end of the continuum are those who assert that these processes make sense only in the context of domain-specific content. Resnick (1987) and Glaser (1984, 1985) are perhaps the most widely recognized proponents of this perspective. Their position on the extending and refining operations described in this chapter would probably be that students should be given such tasks only to learn about content. The operations should not be taught as skills in themselves.

The Dimensions of Learning model combines the best of both views, although there is a strong bias toward the Resnick and Glaser end of the continuum. Because the extending and refining operations are intended as activities to help students deepen their knowledge of content, they should be presented to students as tasks that involve content-specific declarative and procedural information. There is, however, one situation in which it might be advantageous to teach the steps or heuristics involved in these operations: when students cannot perform or are having difficulty with a task for reasons other than their knowledge of the content involved. This might occur frequently in the lower elementary grades. I have witnessed situations where students were fully knowledgeable about the content involved, but had extreme difficulty with extending and refining tasks. The difficulty was alleviated when the teacher explained the processes involved and then demonstrated them for students.

One way of ensuring that students understand and can effectively use the extending and refining operations is to use Beyer's direct instruction approach with one important modification: the processes should not be presented in a content-free manner. That is, the teacher should outline the explicit steps in each process and use the subject being studied to give students practice in using the steps. In this way, students receive a detailed and clear demonstration of the processes without taking time or energy away from the curriculum.

Another way of increasing the probability that students can use the extending and refining processes is to initially use tasks that are structured in such a way as to make the process explicit. Here is an example of a "process explicit" abstraction task:

> Bees, termites, and ants live in tightly structured social groups with strict rules governing behavior and roles within the group. Examine the rules that govern one of these societies, considering especially rules involving leadership and rank, work, living space, cooperation, competition, taking care of and educating the young, and continuation of the group. Relate the patterns that you have identified in the insect kingdom to the patterns that you see in human social groups (such as those in tribes, cities, small towns, or work in large companies or factories).

This task is structured so that students are presented with the literal information on which they are to focus (rules in a specific insect society regarding leadership, rank, work, and so on) and the general situation to which the information is to be abstracted (human societies). The part of the abstraction process left to students is to identify the abstract or general pattern. In short, the abstraction process is built into the task.

For some students in some situations, it is advantageous, if not necessary, to receive explicit guidance in the processes and general rules underlying the operations for extending and refining knowledge. Theoretically, this guidance should help students transfer their use of these skills to other content areas, but it is common knowledge that the research on transfer is discouraging for people seeking to develop strategies that will help students transfer skills (Hayes 1981). After describing a study in which a subject was unable to transfer his skill in memorizing digits to the task of memorizing letters, Anderson (1990) noted that "this is an almost ridiculous extreme of what is becoming a depressing pattern in the development of cognitive skills. This is that these skills can be quite narrow and fail to transfer to other activities" (p. 284).

Even in light of these conclusions, there is some hope. Transfer appears to occur under two conditions, similar elements and explicit cueing. E. L. Thorndike, in a series of experiments, established the theory of similar elements, which states that the more two processes have in common the higher the probability of transfer (Thorndike 1906, Thorndike and Woodworth 1901). That is, the knowledge involved in process A would transfer to process B as long as process B had similar steps or component parts. Actually, Thorndike said that the processes had to have identical elements, but in later studies researchers showed that the elements simply had to be similar (Singly and Anderson 1989).

Even when processes contain similar elements, transfer usually doesn't occur without cueing. For example, Gick and Holyoak (1980, 1983) found that with a cue, 75 percent of students could transfer the process learned in one task to another. In contrast, only 30 percent of their subjects performed the transfer without the cue. In other words, students had to be explicitly reminded to use the strategies they had been taught.

In summary, for transfer to occur, the skill or process used in one task must be very similar to that in the transfer task and students must be reminded to use the strategy. Fortunately, these conditions are easily met by the extending and refining operations described in this chapter. For example, the process of comparison taught in science will be the same as the process of comparison taught in social studies except for the content used. The process of classification taught in mathematics will be the same as that taught in literature except for the content used. Once students learn the eight extending and refining operations, they can use them in any class, provided they are reminded to use them. Using the names of the processes—comparison, classification, induction, deduction, and so on—can be the cue for the processes that have been taught. Arthur Costa and I (1991) believe that teachers should regularly use the names of analytic skills in the classroom as part of a "language of thinking" shared by teacher and students. Carolyn Hughes, one of the initiators of the current emphasis on teaching thinking skills in American classrooms, has long asserted that from the primary grades on, students should be taught the names of the reasoning skills we want them to use.

Planning for Extending and Refining Knowledge

Just as a teacher plans activities to help students acquire and integrate declarative and procedural knowledge, so too must she plan to help students extend and refine their knowledge. Again, let's consider Ms. Conklin's planning for the unit on weather.

Ms. Conklin's Planning for Dimension 3

Ms. Conklin is pleased with the activities she has identified to help students acquire and integrate the information about weather. Surely all these different experiences will help students make the information about weather part of their knowledge base. But she wants them to go much further. She would like to help students think deeply about the content. First she has to consider which information to focus on. She soon finds that this isn't an easy decision. Even though she has been fairly specific about which information to emphasize in the various learning experiences, she must now be even more specific. She decides that three areas are good candidates for extending and refining activities:

- The events leading up to a tornado
- How we forecast the weather
- Air pressure

In choosing extending and refining activities, she asks herself what kind of activities would suit the content. Her thinking goes something like this: "Let's see. I think it's important that they understand that the process of a tornado forming has some unique characteristics. Maybe comparing it with how a hurricane forms would bring out those unique characteristics. But what should I have them do to extend their knowledge about weather forecasting?" As she makes decisions about extending and refining activities, she records them in the unit planning guide (see Figure 4.9).

FIGURE 4.9
Unit Planning Guide for
Dimension 3: Extending and Refining Knowledge

Information	Compare	Classify	Induce	Deduce	Analyze Errors	Support	Abstract	Analyze Perspectives
Sequence of events of tornado	Compare tornado with hurricane							
Forecasting Weather			Students will draw conclusions about weather people					
Air Pressure Rise and Drop							Students will generate abstract pattern + relate to another process in nature	

When Ms. Conklin is done, she pauses for a moment to reconsider her decisions. The more she thinks about the activities she has identified, the more excited she becomes. "There are some things here they can really get their teeth into. But I'm going to have to give them a lot of guidance."

Ms. Conklin's planning illustrates two basic decisions involved in planning for Dimension 3:

1. What information will be extended and refined? Not all information must be analyzed in depth. The sheer amount of information available in most subjects makes that impossible. In 1982, John Naisbitt pointed out the futility of trying to keep up with the growth of information:

> • Between 6,000 and 7,000 scientific articles are written each day.
> • Scientific and technical information now increases 13 percent per year, which means it doubles every 5.5 years.
> • But the rate will soon jump to perhaps 40 percent per year because of new, more powerful information systems and an increasing population of scientists. That means that data will double every twenty months (Naisbitt 1982, p. 24).

Even though Naisbitt's predictions have not been entirely accurate, his essential message has proved true: Information continues to grow geometrically. It is impossible to know everything about a subject and even more foolhardy to try to teach everything about a subject. The renowned mathematician John von Neumann put it succinctly when he noted that a century ago it was possible to understand all of mathematics, but by 1950 even the most well-informed mathematician could have access to only 10 percent of the knowledge of this field (in Gardner, p. 149). The implication, then, is that educators must specify the information to be analyzed in depth. Of all the information covered in her unit on weather, Ms. Conklin has decided to focus on three basic pieces.

2. What activities will be used to help students extend and refine their knowledge? The important rule of thumb when selecting extending and refining tasks is to "let the content select the tasks"; that is, activities should naturally fall out of the content. For example, comparing the events leading up to a tornado with those leading up to a hurricane seems to be a natural way of extending and refining knowledge about tornadoes. The activity of comparison, then, fits well with that particular content, whereas the activity of analyzing errors or constructing support would not seem to fit as well. I have witnessed some disastrous results when teachers have tried to fit the content to the task, rather than the task to the content. Such tasks are usually clumsy, uninspiring, and not very effective. On the other hand, when teachers think of the eight categories of tasks described in this chapter as a menu from which to choose, the results can be very exciting. In some units, they use a little induction and analysis of perspectives because these go well with the content. In other units, comparison and abstraction may better complement the unit. What's most important is that the task help students better understand what they are learning.

5

❖

DIMENSION 4
Using Knowledge
Meaningfully

❖

Generally, we acquire and integrate knowledge because we want or need to use it. For instance, when I was a graduate student with little money to spare, I learned a great deal about automobile engines because I wanted to save money by doing my own tune-ups (since then, I've learned that's what grown sons are for). And recently, I learned a lot about stereos because I wanted to make an intelligent decision about buying one. In short, we learn best when we need knowledge to accomplish some goal. It's important to note that the extending and refining tasks described in Chapter 4 are not usually the focus of goals. People don't often compare just for the purpose of comparing, they don't abstract simply for the pleasure of abstracting. Some kinds of tasks, however, do represent common goals—common ways we use knowledge meaningfully. They are decision making, investigation, experimental inquiry, problem solving, and invention.

Decision Making

Decision making is the process of answering such questions as "What is the best way to . . . ?" or "Which of these is most suitable . . . ?" It is a process that people of all ages use throughout their lives—usually without thinking much about it. Used in the classroom, however, it is an excellent way to improve learning. To find out how decision making can be used in the classroom, let's look at Ms. Haas' class.

Ms. Haas' Class

The students in Ms. Haas' class have been studying the 1960s. So far, they have really enjoyed the unit. They especially liked watching film clips from *Easy Rider* and a documentary about Woodstock. Ms. Haas has enjoyed the unit too because it made her remember her younger days. She even brought in some of her headbands, bell-bottoms, and love beads that were her uniform at Berkeley. She thinks her students know the people of that era well and some of the issues that shaped the times.

One day a student asks who was the most influential person of the 1960s. Ms. Haas thinks for a moment. "Before I give you my answer, give me yours," she says. One student yells out, "Timothy Leary." "Why?" Ms. Haas asks. Before the student can answer, another student says, "No, it had to be JFK." Ms. Haas sees an opportunity. "OK, let's not answer it right now," she says, "let's take some time." Just then the bell rings, giving her until the next day to plan. She decides to turn her students' interest into a project.

When she meets the class the next day she doesn't have to remind students of the previous discussion. They ask, "Who was the most influential person?" She doesn't answer but instead says, "Let's try something. Pretend that you are on a committee for *Time* magazine, which is publishing an issue commemorating the decade of the 1960s. The cover of this issue will feature the person of that decade. Your job is to decide which person should be selected and justify your decision to the publishers by listing the people that you considered, the criteria you used, and how you rated each person."

We make decisions every day. Most are rather trivial and don't involve a great deal of thought, like where to go for lunch or what movie to see. Some decisions, however, can greatly affect our lives and others'. It is when we make these decisions that we involve ourselves deeply in the content surrounding them. For example, John F. Kennedy was engaged in decision making while he was trying to determine what to do about the Soviets' shipping nuclear missiles to Cuba. In effect, he was asking himself, "What is the best course of action to take for the American people?" According to some accounts of that decision, Kennedy and his advisory committees studied the situation in depth. Similarly, from August 1990 to January 15, 1991, President Bush was engaged in decision making when he was trying to identify the best course of action for the United States in the conflict between Iraq and Kuwait.

There are several decision-making models, including those by Wales, Nardi, and Stager (1985), Halpern (1984), and Ehrenberg, Ehrenberg, and Durfee (1979). Analyzing these models reveals that decision making typically involves a situation in which you must select among two or more alternatives. At the outset, these two or more alternatives commonly are equally appealing or, at least, it is not immediately apparent which is the most appealing. Consequently, to make your selection you first identify what you want from the situation. In more formal terms, you identify the "criteria" or "outcomes" you wish to incorporate in your final selection. For example, during the Cuban missile crisis, Kennedy might have considered the following criteria or outcomes:

- Ensure the long-term safety of the United States.
- Exhibit the appearance of power.
- Avoid forcing military action between the United States and the Soviet Union.

When decision making is done systematically, the next step is to identify the importance of each of the possible outcomes. Kennedy might have concluded that ensuring the long-term safety of the United States and avoiding aggression between the United States and the Soviet Union were high priorities, but appearing powerful was not. Some models of decision making suggest that perceived importance of criteria should be quantified. For example, a weight of 3 could indicate that a criterion is very important; a weight of 2, moderately important; and a weight of 1, not very important. Using this process, Kennedy might have given a weight of 3 to the first and third outcomes and a weight of 1 to the second outcome.

The next step is to identify the alternatives to be considered. Kennedy may have been considering these alternative actions:

1. Blockade Cuba, but do not announce what actions will be taken if the blockade is broken.
2. Blockade Cuba and threaten to sink the ships if the blockade is broken.
3. Allow ships to enter Cuba and threaten to invade the country if the missiles are installed.
4. Allow ships to enter Cuba and do not announce any kind of retaliation.

Once alternative actions have been considered, the outcomes are referenced against the alternative actions. That is, the extent to which each alternative action can bring about each desired outcome is identified. Again, some theorists recommend that this relationship be quantified. A decision matrix like that in Figure 5.1 is a useful tool for such quantification.

Figure 5.1 indicates that the first alternative has a moderate probability of affecting outcome A (it has a weight of 2). Alternative 2 has a high probability of affecting outcome A (it has a weight of 3), and so on. As you can see in this figure, if the decision maker multiplies the "alternative weights" by the "outcome weights" and adds up the products for each alternative, he can reach a quantitative decision.

As the example of the Cuban missile crisis illustrates, the decision-making process forces the decision maker to assign priorities to outcomes and analyze the relationships between outcomes and possible alternatives. This is a fairly sophisticated level of analysis.

In the classroom, the decision-making process can be used in a variety of ways in many content areas. Ms. Haas employed the process to help students use the knowledge they had gained about the 1960s in some realistic and intriguing ways. "Who was the most influential person of the 1960s?" is a question that people, especially those who have studied or lived through the 1960s, might realistically ask. The process of answering this question would inevitably make students aware of aspects of the 1960s they would not have understood without tackling such an involved task.

Decision-making tasks can be used in a variety of content areas. Here is an example of a task that might be used in a science class where students are studying nuclear energy and nuclear reactors:

We have learned about three different types of nuclear reactors. We have also studied the resources and environment nuclear reactors require. Assume you are on a panel charged to select the type of nuclear reactor that will be built in the state and where it will be built. Make your selection of both the type of reactor and the site where it should be built. Your report should include the following items:

• The criteria you used to determine the type of reactor to build and why you used those criteria.
• The extent to which each reactor measured up to each of your criteria.
• The alternative sites you considered.
• The criteria you used to assess the sites.
• The extent to which each site measured up to your criteria.
• Your final selection.

FIGURE 5.1
Decision Matrix

Outcomes	**Alternative Actions**			
	1. Blockade Cuba. No mention of action.	2. Blockade Cuba. Threaten to sink ships.	3. No blockade. Threaten to invade if missiles are installed	4. No blockade. No threat.
A. Ensure long-term safety of United States. [3]	2 X 3=6 [2]	3 X 3=9 [3]	1 X 3=3 [1]	1 X 3=3 [1]
B. Establish appearance of power. [1]	1 X 1=1 [1]	3 X 1=3 [3]	2 X 1=1 [2]	1 X 1=1 [1]
C. Avoid aggression between United States and Soviet Union. [3]	2 X 3=6 [2]	1 X 3=3 [1]	2 X 3=6 [2]	3 X 3=9 [3]
	13	15	10	13

Investigation

There are three basic types of investigation. *Definitional investigation* involves answering such questions as "What are the defining characteristics of . . . ?" or "What are the important features of . . . ?" *Historical investigation* involves answering such questions as "How did this happen?" and "Why did this happen?" And *projective investigation* involves answering such questions as "What would happen if . . . ?" and "What would have happened if . . . ?"

All three types of investigation can be used in a variety of classroom situations. To illustrate, let's consider the examples of Ms. Whisler, Ms. McCombs, and Mr. Kendall, whose classrooms depict the use of definitional, historical, and projective investigation respectively.

Ms. Whisler's Class
(Definitional Investigation)

For the past two units, Ms. Whisler and her students have been studying the various ages in history. They have just finished studying the Renaissance. As Ms. Whisler was summarizing what the class has learned so far, one student asked, "Exactly what is an age?" When she tried to respond, Ms. Whisler realized that she really didn't have a good answer. She knew historians have identified specific ages—the Renaissance, the Dark Ages, the Age of Discovery—but she wasn't really sure how to define an age in general. As a group, Ms. Whisler and her students decided they would like to answer the question "What are the characteristics of an age?" Ms. Whisler explained that in answering this question, they should try to determine the characteristics that define an age in general terms and then look at a few specific ages and see if the characteristics really fit. Ms. Whisler also encouraged students to identify the confusions that exist about the concept of an age: "If we're asking what an age is, other people must be too. Let's see if we can clear up some of the confusion."

Ms. McCombs' Class
(Historical Investigation)

Ms. McCombs' 4th grade class has been studying dinosaurs. The textbook explains that the dinosaurs died because of severe changes in climate. One student who has been interested in dinosaurs since she was five years old says, "That's not why the dinosaurs died. I read that it was because a big comet hit the earth and they all died at once." Ms. McCombs says, "Well, you're right. There are a number of explanations for why the dinosaurs died." Rather than describe the various theories, Ms. McCombs decides to turn the question of why the dinosaurs died into a research project. She writes the question on the board: "Why did the dinosaurs die?" She explains to students that they can work in groups or on their own. They have to come up with an answer that satisfies them, but their answer also must take into account other explanations; they must describe why their answer is the best. One of the students asks, "Where do we start?" Ms. McCombs replies, "Anywhere you want. Let's go talk to the librarian to see what we have available to help you."

Mr. Kendall's Class
(Projective Investigation)

One day while studying the concept of the "greenhouse effect," a student in Mr. Kendall's science class asks, "What will happen if the greenhouse effect is true? I mean, what will really happen if the temperature of the entire earth goes up?" Mr. Kendall throws the question right back at the students: "What do you think?" To his surprise, they get into a lively and very heated discussion. Some students say they have heard that if the temperature goes up more than 3°F the polar caps will melt and all the coastlines will be flooded; New York and Los Angeles will be under water. Another student says she heard that for the polar ice caps to melt, the temperature would have to go up at least 10°F and that would be impossible even in the worst conditions. The debate lasts until the end of the period.

The next day students want to continue the debate as soon as class starts again. Mr. Kendall responds, "We need more information. Let's investigate this issue. What would happen if the greenhouse effect were an undeniable reality?" Mr. Kendall makes the question more specific by identifying some assumptions they will work under, the most important of which is that within ten years the overall temperature of the entire planet will rise by 3°F and then remain stable for a thirty-year period due to the corrective efforts of people around the world. Students have a week to work on the question in small groups. Mr. Kendall tells students that in their reporting they should explain the confusions about this issue and describe the conflicting viewpoints.

Definitional Investigation

As Ms. Whisler's example illustrates, definitional investigation involves identifying the defining characteristics of a concept for which such characteristics are unknown or, at least, not readily apparent. Although students had been studying various ages, neither they nor Ms. Whisler was sure about the defining characteristics of an age. Additionally, there was no place they could go to easily obtain that information. In most fields, definitional investigation is a continuing process. For example, people are still investigating how to define the concept "legally dead." What is the defining characteristic of that concept? Is it that all vital signs have stopped or is it that the brain's higher-order functions have ceased? In fact, many of the current issues facing modern society are issues that can be explored using definitional investigation. Consider the issues of abortion and defamation of the American flag. We can phrase each of these issues in the formal terms of definitional investigation:

• *Abortion*. What are the defining characteristics of a person who has the rights of an individual in our society? Does a fetus have such rights? Are these rights protected from the moment of conception? (And how do we confine conception?) Are they protected from the moment of birth?

• *Defamation of the American flag*. What are the defining characteristics of freedom of speech? Does it extend to the defamation of the American flag?

Definitional investigation is basic to an advancing society. It is a powerful tool used to make important distinctions about evolving concepts. In the classroom, it can be used in virtually every content area where understanding concepts is important. Here is an example of a definitional investigation task that might be used in a social studies class:

> Identify a past or present amendment to the U.S. Constitution that has caused controversy or confusion. Tell what is known or agreed upon about this amendment and explain where the confusion or contradiction exists. What do you think is the intent of this amendment and how could this amendment be reworded to reflect your views and clear up the confusion?

Historical Investigation

Historical investigation involves identifying why or how some past event occurred. This was the type of investigation used in Ms. McCombs' class. Much of what is called investigative reporting falls into the category of historical investigation. For example, Bob Woodward and Carl Bernstein were involved in historical investigation when they uncovered and reported the events surrounding the Watergate break-in. Similarly, the researchers and theorists who have been trying to unravel the mystery surrounding the assassination of John F. Kennedy have been involved in historical investigation.

Historical investigation is basic to our attempts to understand the past. Of course, there are many content areas in which such a perspective is a driving force. History, literature, and anthropology are to a great extent driven by such questions as "Why didn't Hitler heed the advice of his generals about the inevitability and severity of the Normandy invasion?" "Why did Hemingway commit suicide?" "How did Neanderthal man die out?" There are also many opportunities for historical investigation in fields that, on the surface, do not appear to have an historical bent. For example, here is an historical investigation task that a high school calculus teacher gave to her class:

> We now know that Newton discovered calculus years before Leibniz did, but Newton published his work much later than Leibniz. A major row ensued over who had been first. As the row grew, Leibniz made the mistake of appealing to the Royal Society to resolve the dispute. Newton, as president of the society, appointed an "impartial" committee to investigate the issue. The report from the committee officially accused Leibniz of plagiarism. Some people say Newton wrote the report himself. Your task is to find out the truth about this incident. Identify the conflicting theories and defend the one that you think is the most credible.

Projective Investigation

Projective investigation involves identifying what will happen if some future event occurs or what would have happened if some past event had occurred. Projective investigation deals with the hypothetical. The current debate about what will happen if more of the rain forests in Brazil are cut down and the debate over what will happen if the ozone layer continues to erode are examples of projective investigation. In school, we can readily use projective investigation in content areas that deal with hypothetical past or future situations. For example, here is an investigation that might be done in a high school sociology class:

> The notion that some countries are more "developed" than others implies that one country's future may be understood as, in part, the reenactment of another country's past. Select some aspect of development for which this might hold true (cultural, military, spiritual,

etc.). Working within the aspect of development you have selected, describe those changes in a developing country that you believe you can predict with some confidence. Identify those areas that would be least predictable. Finally, describe the ways in which the aspect of development you have selected can be better understood from the perspective of more developed countries, and in what ways that perspective can be misleading.

All three types of investigation involve several common elements. For one, they involve identifying what is known or commonly accepted about the concept, past event, or hypothetical event being studied. Students performing Ms. Whisler's project on the characteristics of an age would first have to identify what is already known or accepted about the concept of historic ages. Ms. McCombs' students would have to identify what is known and accepted about the disappearance of dinosaurs, and Mr. Kendall's students, what is known and accepted about the greenhouse effect. At this identifying stage, students should use primary source materials as much as possible so they can get undiluted information. For example, if students were doing an historical investigation about why Hemingway committed suicide, they should be encouraged to read his letters or his relatives' accounts of him.

Perhaps the most important part of any type of investigation is identifying contradictions or confusions. Note that Ms. Whisler, Ms. McCombs, and Mr. Kendall all stressed that students should highlight the confusions and contradictions surrounding their topics. It is the desire to resolve confusions and contradictions that usually moves a person to investigate.

The last element all types of investigation have in common is the solutions to the contradictions and confusions previously identified. The importance of identifying confusions and contradictions and then offering and justifying solutions cannot be emphasized enough. These components are the life force of investigation. Without them, the process is simply a matter of collecting information and reporting it. This was dramatically illustrated to me when my daughter Carmen was required to do a "report" on the Exodus. She approached it as a simple matter of collecting information from various encyclopedias, the Bible, and some books from the library. She was not very enthusiastic about the project until she found a contradiction in some of the materials she was using. Specifically, she found that in most accounts of the Exodus, Moses was credited with parting the waters of the Red Sea so that the enslaved Jewish nation could escape the Egyptian army. When the army tried to pass through the parted waters, they were drowned. In one of the books she had checked out of the library, however, the description of the incident stated that Moses led the Hebrew people across the *Reed Sea,* which was a shallow marshland. When the Egyptian army tried to cross, their heavy chariots and machinery became bogged down in the mire.

When Carmen asked me about the contradiction, I explained that there are various theories about the literal interpretation of biblical stories. Some believe they describe actual history, whereas others believe they are fictional stories intended to teach important truths. Carmen became intensely interested in this issue and we talked at length about the possibilities. Unfortunately, her enthusiasm was not funneled back into her project because the project was not set up in such a way as to focus on the contradictions and confusions surrounding the topic.

In short, the potential power of definitional, historic, and projective investigation is immense if the investigations are structured in a way that forces students to provide and justify solutions for confusions and contradictions.

Experimental Inquiry

Experimental inquiry is the process we engage in when answering such questions as "How can I explain this?" and "Based on my explanation, what can I predict?" To explore how experimental inquiry might be used in the classroom, let's look at Ms. Isaac's class.

Ms. Isaac's Class

To make the classroom environment a little brighter, Ms. Isaac had brought in different types of plants and flowers and let her students choose where to place them in the room. One vine was placed in a small cubbyhole under a shelf where there wasn't much light. After two weeks, one student noticed that the plant had grown in an odd fashion. It hadn't grown straight up, as the other plants had, but grew out sideways and took two or three turns until its outermost vines reached the window and the sunlight. Then it grew straight up.

When students asked why this had happened, Ms. Isaac seized the opportunity for a science lesson. She first had students generate their own explanations for the phenomena. Some thought it was because plants need light. Others thought it was because they need fresh air. Although Ms. Isaacs was tempted, she didn't correct any of their explanations. She simply asked, "Why do you think that might be?" Then she asked students to make a prediction based on their explanations and set up an experiment to test their prediction. She was amazed at what they came up with.

The next few days were spent setting up the experiments. Some students even brought in their parents, who had become interested when their children began asking related questions at the dinner table. It took two weeks to set up and conduct all the experiments. During that time, the children could hardly wait to finish their other lessons so they could check the progress of their studies. When the experiments were over, the children reevaluated their initial explanations. Three students whose original explanations contained the premise that plants will grow toward the light had the most success with their experiments. As a class, they decided that this principle seemed the most accurate. They all wanted to set up another experiment to reaffirm the principle.

Of course, the approach described in Ms. Isaac's class is the basis of modern science. The process of observing phenomena, generating explanations, making predictions, and then testing those predictions is frequently referred to as the scientific method. This type of thinking has changed the world. Prior to the scientific revolution some four centuries ago, physical and psychological phenomena were explained by deductive reasoning from "revealed truth." Observations were not necessary because the world could be explained by reasoning from what was known. In fact, anyone who challenged known "truth" did so at a great risk. As the renowned physicist Stephen Hawking (1988) explains, Copernicus anonymously circulated his theory that the sun was the center of the universe because he feared being branded a heretic. Nearly a century later, Galileo was placed under house arrest for the last eight years of his life by a clergyman protecting revealed truth, because Galileo publicly supported the Copernican hypothesis (Gilovich 1991).

In its most basic form, experimental inquiry involves observing, analyzing, predicting, testing, and reevaluating. For instance, a student might first *observe* that water in a shallow pan left overnight evaporates. The student would then *analyze* the event in an attempt to explain what happened (e.g., the water evaporated because it was exposed to dry air). Based on this analysis, the student would *predict* what might happen under certain conditions (e.g., the lower the humidity, the quicker water evaporates). The student would then *test* his prediction by setting up an experiment. Finally, based on the outcome of his experiment, the student would *reevaluate* his original explanation.

Many people assume that experimental inquiry is the standard operating procedure of science classes in U.S. public schools. Unfortunately, this is not true. In a recent report on common practices in American classrooms, NAEP reported that only 53 percent of the students surveyed said they daily or weekly do science experiments with others and 18 percent said they never do. Only 29 percent said they daily or weekly do experiments by themselves and 46 percent said they never do experiments by themselves (Mullis et al. 1990).

If experimental inquiry is rare in science classrooms, it is virtually nonexistent in other classrooms. This need not be the case; experimental inquiry can and should be used in all content areas. In my teacher workshops, I often say this, and I usually see puzzled looks on teachers' faces. Social studies or literature teachers usually react by saying that experimental inquiry is meant to explain physical phenomena. What these educators overlook is that experimental inquiry is also the preferred method of explaining psychological phenomena or human reactions. The realization that experimental inquiry can be used to explain human reactions opens the door for its uses across all disciplines.

For example, in a literature class, a student might become aware that she is easily confused by the writing of Faulkner. This represents the observational phase of experimental inquiry as it applies to psychological phenomena: noting a reaction in yourself or in others. During the analysis phase of the experimental inquiry process, the student would try to determine why she reacts this way to Faulkner. She might conclude that it is Faulkner's use of long, syntactically complex sentences that confuses her. During the prediction phase, she might hypothesize that information written in long sentences is more difficult to understand than information written in short sentences. During the testing phase, she would set up an activity to test her hypothesis. She might write two short essays covering exactly the same content, but write one essay using long, syntactically complex sentences and write the other using short, syntactically simple sentences. She could then test classmates on the content, perhaps by using an essay question. The student scientist would then evaluate the essay answers to determine which group best understood the content—the students who read the information presented in short sentences or those who read the information presented in longer sentences. Finally, during the reevaluation phase, the student would reexamine her initial conclusions, either affirming or altering them based on the results of her activity. The results here might indicate that when sentences become too syntactically simple, the information they convey is also difficult to comprehend. Hence, she might conclude that information is more easily understood by the reader when the syntax used to express it is moderately complex.

Experimental inquiry, then, can be applied powerfully to almost any subject. The first example below is an experimental inquiry task that might be used in a physics class. The second is an experimental inquiry task that might be used in a social studies class.

Example 1

You've observed that when you are descending in an elevator, you feel heavier as the elevator comes to a stop. Do you suddenly gain weight, then lose it again? How can you explain this feeling? Based on your understanding of the principles involved, make a prediction about the extent to which a given object will have a different weight in a specific situation. Set up an experiment that will test your prediction, carry out the experiment, and then describe whether your experiment proved or disproved your hypothesis. Discuss the extent to which the principles you've described still hold true.

Example 2

The people who entered adulthood in the 1960s are now in their forties. Some would say the 1960s have had no long-term effects on these people. Others would argue that, in subtle ways, the experiences of the 1960s are influencing the way these people are living their lives today. Try to determine what effects the experiences of the 1960s are having on life in the 1990s. Test your hypotheses by applying them to a number of people who were in their early twenties in 1960.

Problem Solving

Problem solving involves answering such questions as "How will I overcome this obstacle?" or "How will I reach my goal but still meet these conditions?" At its core, it is the process of achieving a goal that is blocked by some obstacle or limiting condition. But this is a fairly narrow definition of problem solving. In a very broad sense, any attempt to achieve a goal can be characterized as problem solving. In fact, Anderson (1982, 1983) and others have built computer programs that can "learn" using an algorithm that assumes all learning is problem solving. Conceptualizing problem solving in the narrow sense of overcoming overt obstacles to a goal, however, allows teachers to devise tasks that reinforce a specific and highly important type of thinking. Roger von Oech makes this point in his book *A Whack on the Side of the Head* (1983). Fundamentally, he says that we become truly creative when we are forced to perform routine operations in a new way. To explore how problem solving can be used in the classroom, let's look at Mr. Grossman's class.

Mr. Grossman's Class

Mr. Grossman's class has just finished studying the preservative effects of salt on food. In fact, they spent two weeks studying the exact chemical reactions that create the preservative effect. One student asks, "How could people have preserved food without salt?" Another student replies, "They could have used ice." Mr. Grossman points out that in the days when people used salt as a preservative, they had no way of keeping ice from melting. Another student asks, "What if they hadn't found out about salt? Was there any alternative?" Mr. Grossman says, "You know, you're raising a very interesting question. How could we accomplish the same preservative effects of salt without using salt or refrigeration? Let's make it even tougher. How could we achieve the preservative effect of salt without using any of its basic components—sodium or chlorine—and without using refrigeration of any sort?" At first the students think Mr. Grossman is joking, but then they realize he really wants them to answer this question. One student asks, "Can it be done?" Mr. Grossman responds, "I don't know, let's give it a try."

It is the type of thinking that springs from Mr. Grossman's challenge that has led to some of our great inventions. The powerful thinking skills program *Odyssey of the Mind* (Gourley 1981, Gourley and Micklus 1989) poses similar problems that require students to achieve goals under specific conditions or constraints. Here are some examples:

- Present the Gettysburg address in a new artificial language. You cannot use any English words or conventions. Be prepared to explain the words and any rules you have created for your language.

- Create a freestanding structure that is as tall as possible using only playing cards and masking tape.

- Build as complex a structure as possible inside a clear plastic, two-liter container for soft drinks without cutting or altering the container in any way. Entry to the inside of the container should be only through the mouth of the plastic bottle.

The process of solving a problem begins with specifying a goal. For example, if you get up one morning and find that your car won't start, you have a problem. In this situation, the goal is obvious: getting to work. The next step might be described as identifying the constraint. Here, the constraint is that your usual method of transportation is not available. An important part of problem solving is identifying alternative ways of accomplishing the goal. In this example, that means determining other modes of transportation: taking a bus, finding a ride with a friend, or riding your bicycle. Finally, problem solving involves selecting an alternative and trying it out.

Teachers can use this process in a wide variety of subjects. An English teacher once related to me the results of asking students to devise a method of signaling complete thoughts and questions in oral language without using pitch (conventionally we lower pitch to signal the end of a complete thought and raise pitch to signal a question). The teacher explained that this task led students to explore aspects of language they would otherwise never have considered. For example, one group of students began a study of the nature and function of inflection in various languages. They found that one tribe of people signals complete thoughts by making clicking noises with the tongue, so they adapted a variation of these conventions to solve the problem.

Similarly, an elementary mathematics teacher described to me a problem she gave students that greatly enhanced their understanding of the conventions of long division. She explained that her students were quite good at performing long division using the standard method in which the divisor is placed next to the dividend on a horizontal plane:

$$357 \overline{)\, 9723}$$

As a problem-solving task, she asked students to devise a method of performing long division in which the divisor is placed on top of the dividend:

$$\frac{357}{9723}$$

The teacher noted that while formulating their solutions to the problem, students carefully considered the importance of keeping track of place values.

We saw earlier that experimental inquiry is not limited to science, and, likewise, problem solving is not limited to mathematics. Problem solving can help students explore issues in virtually any content area. Here is an example of a problem-solving task that might be used in a social studies class:

> You are the wagon master of a wagon train of pioneer families on its way from Ohio to California. Unfortunately, none of the wagons can go through water and your bridge- and raft-building capabilities on the trail are extremely limited. It is your job to find a new route for

the wagon train or a process that will eliminate taking the wagons through water. Your journey may take as long as you like, but you must consider the effects of the seasons. Trace your route on a map and describe the terrain you cross. How far will you go? How much longer is your route than an actual pioneer trail and how much longer would it take?

Invention

Invention is the process of creating something that fills an unmet need or desire. In effect, you are inventing when you attempt to answer such questions as "What would I like to create?" "What is a new way?" "What is a better way?" To explore how invention might be used in the classroom, let's look at Mr. Barlow's class.

Mr. Barlow's Class

Mr. Barlow's class has just come back from a trip to a local housing project (where some of the students live) as part of their unit on current issues in the community. They have been studying how city funds are used to meet local needs. In their field trip, students also visited the various city agencies that provide service to the housing project. During the discussion they have back in the classroom, a couple of students say that although tenants have places they can go for health care and for food and clothing, they have nowhere to go for help with their day-to-day lives, no place where they can air their gripes and talk about the difficulties they're having. The students who live in the projects agree that domestic violence is high and that much of it is a result of tension within families.

Mr. Barlow paraphrases what they are saying: "What you want to do, then, is create a new service. Is that it?" The students agree. "OK, what would it do? What would be its purpose?" Students begin calling out all the things that the new service would provide and Mr. Barlow writes their suggestions on the board. After a while, it becomes obvious that this project is going to take more than one class period. Mr. Barlow says, "I'll give you six days to work together over the next week and a half. Let's see if you can really do it—create an agency, that is. You can work individually, in pairs, in small groups, whatever you like, but you have to come up with a detailed plan for your new agency. Specify what it would do, how much it would cost to make it work, how it would work, and how you would know when it's successful. When we're done, we'll take the plans to our city council."

Mr. Barlow's class was involved in invention, whereas Mr. Grossman's class was involved in problem solving. What is the difference? Basically, both involve creating a product or a process. Mr. Grossman's class was developing something that would have the preservative properties of salt but not use any of the basic elements. Mr. Barlow's class was developing a new service. In problem solving, however, the product or process is created under specific constraints or conditions. Thus, the emphasis is on overcoming a specific obstacle or constraint. You might say that Mr. Grossman's class had very few "degrees of freedom."

In invention, there is usually no obstacle (although the inventor might encounter obstacles along the way); rather, the emphasis is on filling some perceived need by improving on something or creating something totally new. Because of this difference in emphasis, the process of invention is qualitatively different from that of problem solving. Rather than initially focusing on obstacles or constraints, the invention process initially focuses on the product. This involves setting specific standards that will be met. Once standards are set, the inventor, like the problem solver, must work within specifications. The inventor, though, is usually free to change the standards, whereas the problem solver is rarely free to change the constraints.

Once standards or criteria are identified, the inventor's next step is to create a rough sketch or plan. For example, in Mr. Barlow's class students would have to outline how the new service would operate. A sketch or rough description created, the inventor then develops a first draft or working model. If Mr. Barlow's students were to complete the invention process, they would eventually create a working model of their new service—a pilot project, so to speak. This draft or working model then goes through successive revisions until the final product meets the criteria for success that were initially established. This is another major difference between problem solving and invention: the result of invention is a product that has been extensively revised and polished, whereas the result of problem solving is simply the satisfaction of overcoming the constraints.

Invention, then, involves the conception, development, and polishing of a product that meets a perceived need and specific standards established by the inventor. There are thousands of examples of invention. The Wright brothers saw a need for manned flight and set out to meet that need. They established certain standards for their new invention, the most important being that it would carry a full-grown adult over a significant distance. Within the invention process, they were free to change their standards—and by some accounts they did so several times. They also spent a long time refining their product.

Invention is one of the most open-ended and creative tasks that students can be involved in. It can be used in virtually every content area. Here is an example of an invention task that might be used in a home economics class:

> People in wheelchairs have many problems in houses designed for people who are able to maneuver, reach, and stand. Your task is to design a kitchen that is "wheelchair friendly," using any arrangement and materials you think are appropriate. You might want to think about redesigning the appliances, sinks, lighting, layout, access, and storage areas. Develop a detailed model of your kitchen and invite a person in a wheelchair (preferably an adult who cooks and cleans) to critique it and offer suggestions. Revise your design until it meets the standards of utility and efficiency determined by the wheelchair-bound community.

What Makes These Tasks Meaningful?

In this chapter I have asserted that decision making, investigation, experimental inquiry, problem solving, and invention are types of tasks that involve students in the meaningful use of knowledge. But what makes these tasks meaningful? In general, meaningful classroom tasks fall into three categories: application-oriented tasks, long-term tasks, and student-directed tasks.

Application-Oriented Tasks

All the tasks described in this chapter focus on the application of knowledge. Each can be conceptualized as answering specific types of questions. For example, decision making answers the question "What is the best?" Definitional investigation answers questions like "What are the defining characteristics?" These tasks require students to use their knowledge to accomplish specific goals or to apply their knowledge when answering specific questions. Their emphasis is not learning for learning's sake, but learning as a by-product of trying to accomplish something, of trying to answer questions that are common human concerns. This is always the most powerful kind of learning.

Long-Term Tasks

The length of the class period and the length of the course determine the lower and upper limits of long-term tasks in the classroom. In the traditional fifty-minute class period, a long-term task should last at least three classes. It could, however, last as long as the course itself: a quarter, a semester, or a year, depending on the classroom setting. In most classrooms, though, the most practical way to use long-term projects is to tie them to units of instruction. Many teachers break instruction into theme units that last from one to six weeks. Within a unit of instruction, then, a task could last up to six weeks.

Unfortunately, the principle that classroom tasks should be long-term flies in the face of current practice. These learning tasks rarely take even one or two periods to finish; besides that, they are usually directed by the teacher and require little higher-order thinking (Doyle 1983, Fisher and Hiebert 1988). The most common task is probably reading a selection from a textbook and then answering questions at the end of the selection or completing a textbook exercise.

Student-Directed Tasks

The characteristic that is most important if a task is to be called meaningful is the extent to which it is student directed. This means two things: (1) students have control over the construction of the tasks, and (2) students have control over the products generated from the task.

At the very least, students should have control over the construction of tasks: they should identify the questions they would like to answer about the topic they are studying. The teacher and students might first discuss issues that have come up in the unit, but students should then be able to identify questions relating to these issues and construct appropriate tasks. Of course, when an issue of particular importance surfaces, the teacher may still devise tasks for students. And when students are first introduced to the five types of tasks described in this chapter, they will no doubt need a great deal of guidance from the teacher. In general, though, students should have the freedom to create their own tasks and be encouraged to do so.

Students should also have some control over the products generated from the tasks. Generally, outcomes and products in school are limited to written and oral reports (Durst and Newell 1989). That is, students are commonly required to write an essay or make an oral report describing what they have learned. As useful as these methods of presentation are, they exclude other methods of presenting information. Video- or audiotaped reports, newscasts, graphic organizers accompanied by explanations, slide shows, dramatic presentations, demonstrations, debates, and panel discussions are all valid ways of reporting the results of the tasks described in this chapter.

For instance, the students in Ms. Haas' class might have presented the results of their investigation of the most important person of the 1960s in a video or in a debate. And the students in Mr. Kendall's class might have presented the results of their investigation of the greenhouse effect in a newscast or dramatic presentation.

The products of meaningful-use tasks can be expanded even beyond the list presented above if students are allowed and encouraged to develop artifacts along with their tasks. Artifacts are artistic or symbolic representations of affective experiences associated with a task. For example, in a decision-making task about which action would have been best for the United States to take in the conflict between Iraq and Kuwait, a student might develop a sketch to supplement her written report. The written report would be used to communicate the process used in the decision-making task and the conclusions drawn from it, while the artifact (the sketch) would be used to communicate a specific feeling associated with the learner's conclusions. In short, the learner would use the sketch to represent the emotion she had experienced while gathering information for the decision-making task.

Introducing Meaningful-Use Tasks

Because of the complexity of the meaningful-use tasks described in this chapter, students generally need to be taught the critical aspects of the processes underlying the tasks. It is in introducing the meaningful-use tasks that Beyer's (1988) five-step process for teaching a complex process makes sense:

1. The teacher introduces the process by describing and demonstrating the steps of the process, explaining when the process should be used, and naming the process.

2. Students experiment with the strategy using "neutral" content; that is, the teacher provides students with familiar and interesting content, allowing them to focus on the process without the interference of struggling with new or uninteresting content.

3. Students think about what goes on in their minds as they use the process. This may be done in cooperative groups.

4. As a result of their reflection or group discussion, students may make changes in the strategy.

5. Finally, students try out the modified process and again reflect on its use.

If the processes underlying the meaningful-use tasks are not taught in this manner, then teachers should be prepared to guide students through the tasks or to provide them with highly structured tasks. Over time, then, tasks can shift to a more student-structured format.

Planning for the Meaningful Use of Knowledge

To explore the decisions a teacher needs to make when planning for the meaningful use of knowledge, let's look at Ms. Conklin's planning for Dimension 4. We can assume that over the year Ms. Conklin has introduced students to the processes involved in decision making, investigation, experimental inquiry, problem solving, and invention, so she is free to present a variety of options to students.

Ms. Conklin's Planning for Dimension 4

Ms. Conklin is confident of her students' ability to use knowledge meaningfully through decision making, investigation, experimental inquiry, problem solving, and invention, thus she has a wide range of activities she can use in the classroom. She thinks to herself, "What are some big or unresolved issues relating to weather and the information we'll go over in this unit? Are there important decisions to be made? Are there problems that are still unsolved?" She thinks through the questions the meaningful-use tasks address: "Is there an issue about who or what is the best?" "Is there an issue about the defining characteristics of something or why something happened or what would happen if . . . ?"

After a while, Ms. Conklin concludes that the issue of weather forecasting can be explored further; specifically, she thinks that forecasters could create a better way of warning people about tornadoes. And this issue naturally lends itself to an invention project. She knows her students could not possibly invent a warning system in a four-week unit, but they would probably enjoy trying.

Ms. Conklin also identifies another issue: how weather affects people's moods. She decides that she'll present students with an invention task and an experimental inquiry task as possible projects. For the invention task, she'll simply provide some general guidance by giving students the following directions:

> One of the major needs in weather forecasting is being able to warn people about tornadoes as soon as possible. Study this situation and identify an area that is ready for a new invention. Describe what the invention would do and state the standards it should meet. If you can, create a rough outline or plan for how it would work.

For the experimental inquiry project, she sets up a slightly more structured task:

Some people believe that weather and climate affect people's personality or moods.

1. Describe something you have noticed about the relationship between weather or climate and personality or mood. Explain what you think is happening.
2. Make a prediction based on your explanation.
3. Gather information to test your prediction.
4. Describe the extent to which your information agrees with your prediction.
5. Finally, decide what you learned from your study. What were you right about? What were you wrong about? What interesting insights did you have?

Ms. Conklin also wants to make sure that she leaves room for students to create their own tasks. She'll encourage them to make up their own projects using the ones she presents as models.

While putting the tasks together, Ms. Conklin thinks to herself, "These projects would take any one person a long while to finish." She concludes that these projects should be accomplished in cooperative groups. Although she'll allow students to do the projects independently, she'll encourage them to work cooperatively. She also thinks about the various ways students can report what they have learned. Again, she wants to leave open many possibilities. She decides that she will tell students they have four basic ways to report on their work:

- A written report duplicated and distributed to the rest of the students
- An oral report given to the entire class
- A videotaped report
- A newscast

Each of these options will, she knows, require her guidance. For example, she'll have to go over the format for a newscast and the components of a good videotaped report. She thinks it will be worth it, though, because her students will have the chance to express themselves in a personal way.

Ms. Conklin's example illustrates five major decisions involved in planning for Dimension 4, the meaningful use of knowledge:

1. What are the big issues? As in Dimension 3 (extending and refining knowledge), it is important that the content drive the selection of tasks in Dimension 4. A teacher should look for the big issues that naturally stand out in the content. Below are questions a teacher might think about to identify such issues:

Decision Making
- Is there an unresolved issue about who or what is the best?
- Is there an unresolved issue about who or what has the most or least?

Investigation
- Is there an unresolved issue about the defining characteristics or defining features of something? (Definitional)
- Is there an unresolved issue about how or why something occurred? (Historical)
- Is there an unresolved issue about what would happen if . . . or what would have happened if . . . ? (Projective)

Experimental Inquiry
- Is there an unexplained phenomenon (physical or psychological) for which students could generate explanations that can be tested?

Problem Solving
- Is there a situation or process that has some major constraint or limiting condition?
- Is there a situation that could be better understood if constraints or limiting conditions were placed on it?

Invention
- Is there a situation that can or should be improved on?
- Is there something that should be created?

2. How many issues will be considered? On the one hand, the more issues considered, the more options students have for choosing projects. On the other hand, the more options presented, the more familiar students have to be with the various types of meaningful-use tasks. The meaningful-use tasks are complex enough that students usually need a teacher's guidance as they progress through them. Consequently, teachers often initially present only one type of task per unit until students become familiar with all five types of tasks. Only then do units include multiple types of tasks.

3. Who will structure the tasks? Ultimately, students should identify the issues they want to deal with in their projects and the specifics of those tasks. Again, teachers must usually first provide structured activities to help students become familiar with the five types of tasks. Gradually, the teacher can provide less-structured activities and perhaps simply supply examples for students to model their own tasks on. Eventually, the teacher can encourage students to create their own tasks.

4. What types of products will students create? This is one of the most important decisions relating to Dimension 4. Again, the principle is to encourage a variety of options so that students have many opportunities to use their talents and explore their interests. As mentioned previously, teachers typically offer students few options other than oral or written reports for reporting what they have learned. Teachers should think about what other legitimate ways of communicating information would be useful in the unit (e.g., newscasts, simulations, panel discussions). They should also reflect on the aesthetic experiences that could be associated with the topic (e.g., poems, songs, murals).

5. To what extent will students work in cooperative groups? Although cooperative learning is quite compatible with all the dimensions of learning, it is especially suited to the meaningful-use tasks of Dimension 4 because the tasks are complex and lend themselves to such aspects of cooperative learning as individual accountability, positive group interdependence, and group rewards and task specialization (Slavin 1983). These characteristics are discussed in some depth in Chapter 7.

❖ ❖ ❖

In summary, it is within Dimension 4 that students are provided with explicit opportunities to apply knowledge in meaningful ways that allow them to explore personal interests and direct their own learning. They do this in complex tasks such as decision making, investigation, experimental inquiry, problem solving, and invention. Dimension 4 is the heart of the Dimensions of Learning model. Its effectiveness depends on the teacher's careful planning and orchestration and her willingness to turn over control of learning to students.

6

❖

DIMENSION 5
Productive Habits of Mind

❖

We cannot learn (or teach) everything there is to know. Even if we could, we would probably quickly forget it, because human beings tend to forget information they don't use (Wickelgren 1979). For example, during my tenure as a professor at a university, I taught graduate courses in techniques for reading diagnosis. Although it was a complex field, I felt I had a certain mastery of the content and even wrote a textbook on the subject. After not using that information for a decade, though, I was embarrassed recently when I could not answer a simple question on the topic. I had to look up the information in the textbook I had helped write.

Acquiring content knowledge is very important, but perhaps it should not be the most important goal of the education process. Ultimately, it might be better to help students develop mental habits that will help them learn on their own whatever they need or want to know. To explore this idea, let's consider Mr. Nachtigal's class.

Mr. Nachtigal's Class

When students in Mr. Nachtigal's Advanced Placement calculus class talk to students from other classes, they find there are some significant differences between how Mr. Nachtigal runs his class and how other teachers run theirs. The most striking difference is that he doesn't emphasize getting the right answer as much as he emphasizes things like "trying to be accurate in what you do" and "hanging in even when answers aren't immediately apparent." It's not that he doesn't care about students' getting the right answer. It's just that he thinks you can learn almost anything if you've learned to discipline your mind in certain ways.

Mr. Nachtigal introduced this idea the first day of class by giving an unusual speech: "Let's get a few things straight. Your job in this class is to learn. My job is to teach—but not just calculus. My job is to teach you to be good learners, to teach you to be the best you can be." He went on to tell a story about a friend named Dan King with whom he had graduated from college. When Dan was a junior in college, he said that someday he was going to get a Ph.D. in mathematics. His father was a mathematician at the university and he wanted to follow in his footsteps. Dan wasn't terrifically smart but he was very determined. His plans to go to graduate school were interrupted, however, by the war in Vietnam. Dan enlisted and ended up in the special forces. Two weeks before he was to come home, a grenade exploded close by. Dan was blinded.

Mr. Nachtigal saw Dan about a year after he got back to the United States. When he asked Dan what he was going to do, Dan's answer surprised him: "I'm going to get my Ph.D. in mathematics." Mr. Nachtigal didn't say anything, but his immediate reaction was that Dan was setting himself up for a great disappointment. "Math is such a visual subject," he thought. "There's no way he could do such abstract work with his disability." Four years later, with tears in his eyes, Mr. Nachtigal sat through a graduation ceremony and watched Dan receive his Ph.D. in mathematics.

When Mr. Nachtigal asked his students, "How do you think he did it?" one student yelled out, "Guts!" Mr. Nachtigal said, "You're right, but it wasn't just that." What ensued was a fairly long discussion about how people accomplish things in the face of adversity. The class even identified some specific things Dan had probably done:

- Made a plan
- Used his resources
- Changed what he was doing when things weren't working out
- Hung in when the going got tough
- Trusted his own ideas and abilities
- Got people to help him

When the list was completed, Mr. Nachtigal said, "This is what is important to me. Not just calculus. This is what we're going to practice in here."

Mr. Nachtigal's story about Dan King was meant to be inspiring to students. It is a true story. Dan King was a friend of mine in graduate school. He was and is an inspiration to many people, but more important, he dramatically illustrates the power of cultivating specific habits of mind. Dan did not succeed simply because he had a great desire to succeed. Certainly this was necessary to overcome the tremendous obstacles confronting him, but Dan was using what some people call "dispositions of mind" and what the Dimensions of Learning model refers to as "productive habits of mind."

Self-Regulated Thinking and Learning

If you page through a few of the popular "how-to-succeed" books, you'll see that virtually all of them talk about developing good mental habits. For example, Stephen Corey's best-selling book *The Seven Habits of Highly Effective People* (1990) attributes success to seven specific mental habits. On the more academic side, theorists such as Flavell (1976, 1977)) and Brown (1978, 1980) assert that certain mental habits, such as those below, render one's thinking and actions more self-regulated:

- Being aware of your own thinking
- Planning
- Being aware of necessary resources
- Being sensitive to feedback
- Evaluating the effectiveness of your actions

To illustrate, a student might develop a specific plan for an upcoming classroom project. Part of this plan would include identifying necessary resources and establishing milestones. As the student executes the plan, he might occasionally note whether he is getting closer to or further away from his goal and then make corrections as needed.

Critical Thinking and Learning

According to Ennis (1985, 1987, 1989) and Paul and his colleagues (1986, 1989), other mental habits make one's learning more critical in nature:

- Being accurate and seeking accuracy
- Being clear and seeking clarity
- Being open-minded
- Restraining impulsivity
- Taking a position when the situation warrants it

• Being sensitive to others' feelings and level of knowledge

For example, a student might notice that she tends to make bold assertions about topics she's unfamiliar with; as a result, she might decide to begin trying to think about what evidence she has for her position before she speaks. Another student might consciously strive to communicate in a clear fashion, checking to see whether others have understood his communication. It is important to note that the mental habits listed above are not the only aspects of critical thinking. In fact, combining the lists of Paul and Ennis would produce a list of more than twenty mental habits of critical thinking. Additionally, they both list critical thinking "skills and abilities" that include virtually all of the extending and refining activities listed in Chapter 4 of this book. Critical thinking, then, involves a variety of components interacting in complex ways. At the apex of critical thinking, however, is the use of the mental habits described above.

Creative Thinking and Learning

A somewhat different set of dispositions characterizes creativity, another valued form of thinking. According to Amabile (1983) and Perkins (1984, 1985, 1988), creative thinking involves the following mental habits:

• Engaging intensely in tasks even when answers or solutions are not immediately apparent.
• Pushing the limits of your knowledge and abilities.
• Generating, trusting, and maintaining your own standards of evaluation.
• Generating new ways of viewing a situation outside the boundaries of standard conventions.

For instance, a student might notice that she tends to coast through projects, using as little energy as possible. To correct this tendency, she might consciously "push" herself on a project, striving to do the very best she can. She might establish her own standards for a project, even if these vary from more commonly accepted standards. She might also try to see things in ways that are not commonly accepted.

Like critical thinking, creative thinking includes more than the mental habits listed here. Using an activity like abstracting to extend and refine knowledge is also a form of creative thinking. Again, though, at the core of creative thinking are the above mental habits.

The mental habits of self-regulation, critical thinking, and creative thinking permeate virtually every academic task students undertake.

❖

Being, or not being, self-regulated, critical, and creative affects how well students acquire and integrate knowledge. Being, or not being, self-regulated, critical, and creative affects how well students extend and refine knowledge. And it affects how well they make use of their knowledge. To this extent, the habits of mind are like attitudes and perceptions (Dimension 1): when they are negative or weak, they hamper students' ability to learn; when they are positive or strong, they improve students' ability to learn. This is why Dimensions 1 and 5 are depicted as the backdrop for Dimensions 2, 3, and 4 in the Dimensions of Learning diagram in Figure 6.1. Without attention to Dimensions 1 and 5, little effective learning occurs in Dimensions 2, 3, and 4.

Helping Students Develop and Maintain Effective Habits of Mind

The process of helping students develop effective habits of mind is qualitatively different from the processes of helping students develop any of the other dimensions of learning. Unlike positive attitudes and perceptions (Dimension 1), which can be reinforced in a fairly unobtrusive manner by the teacher, the habits of mind must be overtly taught and reinforced. But they do not lend themselves to instruction in explicit strategies as do Dimensions 2, 3, and 4. Rather, the habits of mind must be introduced and then reinforced as they are exhibited.

The habits of mind must be introduced to students because students rarely see these habits of mind being used in the world around them. Few people plan and manage resources well. Few people seek clarity or accuracy. Few people work at the edge, rather than the center, of their competence. In fact, it is rather remarkable how infrequently human beings use these mental habits. After describing some of the dire consequences of ignoring these mental habits, Gilovich (1991) says, "As individuals and as a society, we should be less accepting of superstition and sloppy thinking and should strive to develop those 'habits of mind' that promote a more accurate view of the world" (p. 6).

There are, however, some striking examples of the use of these mental habits that teachers can employ in the classroom. I have seen teachers use specific events from the lives of Gandhi, Abraham Lincoln, George Bush, and others to illustrate one or more of the mental habits. This is what Mr. Nachtigal was doing by relating the story of Dan King: providing students with a real-life example of some of the mental habits. In fact, using stories and literature is probably one of the most popular ways of demonstrating the habits of mind. As Bloome (1991) explains, literature and stories are a society's way of passing on the important values of a culture.

FIGURE 6.1
How the Dimensions of Learning Interact

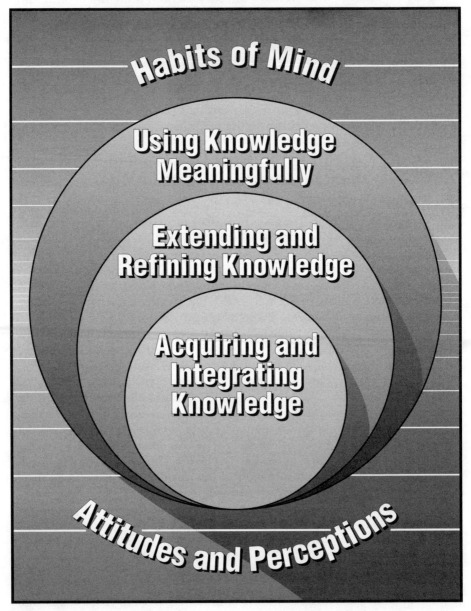

Habits of Mind

Using Knowledge Meaningfully

Extending and Refining Knowledge

Acquiring and Integrating Knowledge

Attitudes and Perceptions

I once observed a very powerful demonstration of how literature can be used to introduce some of the mental habits. The teacher was reading *The Island of the Blue Dolphins* by Scott O'Dell to her 4th grade students. The book is about a young Indian girl named Karana who with her little brother is left on an island off the coast of California when the tribe leaves to avoid a hostile rival tribe. Soon her brother is killed by a pack of wild dogs and Karana must fend for herself for many years. While waiting to be rescued, she builds a house, makes weapons and utensils, finds and preserves food, and eventually adopts the leader of the dog pack, who protects her in a variety of situations. As the teacher read the story, she would periodically stop and ask students to identify the things they admired about Karana and the things that made her successful.

By the time the teacher had finished the book, students had generated a list of nearly thirty characteristics. As I recall, virtually all of the habits of mind described in this chapter, or variations of them, had been identified: Karana had made plans, she had been aware of resources, she had set her own standards, and so on. The teacher then highlighted the habits of mind that were to be the focus for the year. Although this lesson had taken some time and energy, it was a very powerful way of introducing specific habits of mind.

Once students have a basic awareness of the mental habits, the teacher can ask them to find examples among people they know. For example, in a 7th grade classroom in which the teacher had asked students to find examples of people using the mental habit of "hanging in there when answers and solutions aren't apparent," one student returned the next day with a story about how her brother had used that mental habit while trying to make the football team. Another girl told about how her father tried for more than two years to invent a new type of battery, persevering until he finally succeeded.

Another important aspect of introducing students to the habits of mind is asking them to identify specific situations in which each might be useful. Students from a variety of grade levels generated the list of situations in Figure 6.2.

Reinforcement is important too. Teachers should reinforce positive instances of the mental habits. For example, a teacher might notice that a student has paid particular attention to the resources necessary to complete a task, and say to her, "Amina, you're doing a great job of collecting all the material you need before you begin working," thus reinforcing the self-regulatory habit of managing resources. Or a teacher might notice and acknowledge that a student was trying to be particularly accurate: "Bill, I noticed that you looked up the facts in the encyclopedia. Good. That's a great way of making sure you're accurate," reinforcing the critical-thinking habit of seeking accuracy.

FIGURE 6.2
Students' Suggestions of Situations When the Habits of Mind Might Be Useful

Self-Regulation

- Being aware of your own thinking:
  - When you're not doing well on a task, being aware of your own thinking can help you figure out what you're doing wrong.

- Planning:
  - Any time you have to do something that takes a long time and is fairly complex—like completing assignments that take two weeks or even a semester.

- Being aware of necessary resources:
  - Any time you want to make or do something that requires resources. Not having the resources might put limits on what you can do.

- Being sensitive to feedback:
  - When you are doing something that is repetitious (e.g., doing a very long arithmetic problem), being sensitive to feedback helps prevent careless mistakes.

- Evaluating the effectiveness of your actions:
  - When you are doing something new or something you are not very good at, evaluating your actions helps you learn from your mistakes.

Critical Thinking

- Being accurate and seeking accuracy:
  - Whenever you are doing mathematical calculations.
  - Whenever you are doing anything that requires precision.

- Being clear and seeking clarity:
  - Whenever someone is trying to persuade you of something.
  - Whenever you are trying to explain something to someone.
  - Whenever you are not sure of what you are saying or writing.

(continued)

FIGURE 6.2
Students' Suggestions of Situations When the Habits
of Mind Might Be Useful
(continued)

- Being open-minded:
  – Whenever you find yourself immediately rejecting an idea.

- Resisting impulsivity:
  – Whenever you find yourself responding to a question immediately without much thinking prior to your response.

- Taking and defending a position:
  – Whenever you are fairly confident about a specific position and it has not been expressed by someone else.

- Being sensitive to others:
  – Whenever you are dealing with a "touchy" topic that others might feel strongly about.

Creative Thinking

- Engaging intensely in tasks even when answers or solutions are not immediately apparent:
  – Whenever you continue to fail at something that's important to you.

- Pushing the limits of your knowledge and ability.
  – Whenever you find yourself falling into a routine way of doing things.

- Generating, trusting, and maintaining your own standards of evaluation:
  – Whenever you are doing something primarily to please yourself.

- Generating new ways of viewing situations outside the boundaries of standard convention:
  – Whenever you are stuck on a particularly difficult problem.
  – Whenever it is important to consider a variety of options.

For a more formal level of reinforcement, the teacher might use process observers, particularly with meaningful-use tasks (Dimension 4) that are performed in cooperative groups. In this case, one student in each group would be appointed to observe students' use of a specific mental habit. At the end of a class period, the process observer would report on what he observed. For example, he might say, "I saw Bill really trying even though he couldn't figure out the answer."

The Role of Personal Goals

Many of the habits of mind, especially those that relate to self-regulation, can be reinforced quite powerfully as students strive to achieve personal goals. The work in motivation by researchers and theorists like Schunk (1985, 1990) indicates that people are most motivated when they are pursuing personal goals, and it is when they are motivated that they are most likely to use productive habits of mind. In other words, it is when we are trying to accomplish a personal goal that we are most likely to have a need to plan, manage resources, seek accuracy, work at the edge rather than the center of our competence, and so on.

One of my favorite ways of illustrating this point is to relate a story about my son, Todd. Although not a terribly poor student in high school, Todd was certainly not at the top of his class. He took as few academic courses as possible, and his 3.00 GPA was essentially the result of A's in metal shop and phys ed and C's in mathematics and science. In the middle of his junior year, he announced that he was not going to go to college. His logic was that he was not academically oriented (which was true), did not like school (also true), and was talented in auto mechanics (true again). Being the second son of Italian immigrants who stressed education as the way to a better life, I was extremely upset. Of course, I gave many unsolicited speeches about the importance of going to college and the probable effect that not going would have on his life.

At some point during this traumatic period, Todd went to see *Top Gun,* a movie about a modern-day navy aviator. Immediately after seeing the movie, he announced that he wanted to be a fighter pilot. This discouraged me because I believed my son was setting unrealistic goals. A happy turn of events (from my perspective) occurred when my son announced that he was going to college, because "you have to have a college degree to be a fighter pilot." I thought that if I could get him into college under any pretense he would soon abandon the foolishness of trying to be a fighter pilot, given the academic rigors involved. Since Todd had not distinguished himself in science and mathematics in high school, how could he possibly master the advanced mathematics and science he'd need to be a fighter pilot?

To my utter amazement, Todd attacked the science and mathematics courses in college with a fervor I had previously not witnessed in him. He made detailed plans about how to transfer from an open-enrollment community college (the only one he could get into) to one of the best engineering schools in the country. He managed his time and money at a level of detail that bordered on obsession. He strove for accuracy in all his academic classes and surely worked at the edge rather than the center of his competence every day. As I write this book, I can proudly report that Todd is about to graduate magna cum laude with a degree in aerospace engineering from the third best engineering school in the country. Recently, he was inducted into a prestigious engineering fraternity. And along the way he obtained his private pilot's license, receiving a score of 100 on the examination given by the Federal Aviation Administration (the first time in fifteen years anyone from our region received such a high score). Finally (and most important to Todd), he was one of only two candidates from the state accepted into the Aviator's Officer Candidate School of the United States Navy, which is the navy's first and biggest step to becoming a fighter pilot.

In short, when Todd identified and began actively pursuing a goal that truly excited him, he cultivated mental habits he had previously ignored. In retrospect, this makes perfect sense to me. The habits of mind described in this chapter all push against natural human tendencies. The vast majority of people commonly do not like to plan, manage resources, or attend to feedback because of the time and energy involved. We usually do not avoid impulsivity or seek accuracy and clarity because not doing so is easy. For similar reasons, we usually do not work at the edge rather than the center of our competence, persevere even when answers or solutions are not readily available, and so on. But we *do* use these mental habits (which I tend to think of as being at the apex of human thought) when we are striving for something we truly desire.

The implication of this principle is that students should be encouraged to set personal goals—goals that really "turn them on," as aviation did Todd—and then supported in their efforts to accomplish those goals. For example, at the beginning of the school year, students might be asked to identify what they would like to accomplish that year or that semester. Again, the key is to have students identify goals that truly excite them. A teacher, counselor, or some other trusted adult would meet with each student regularly to offer feedback, guidance, and support. This scenario may sound unrealistic, but it is not. It is precisely what takes place at Pioneer Elementary School in Colorado Springs, Colorado, under the direction of Principal Suzanne Lochran. At the beginning of each year, students identify specific academic and personal goals they would like to accomplish, and then they periodically receive feedback, guidance, and support from advisors in the school.

Personal goals are one of the most powerful human motivators. They are the source of a basic life energy. To ignore them within formal education is to ignore a potential tool for teaching productive habits of mind that will serve learners in all kinds of situations throughout life.

The Role of Structured Academic Problems

Another powerful tool for reinforcing many of the habits of mind, especially those dealing with critical and creative thinking, is academic problems. Academic problems are defined here as the well-structured types of problems students commonly encounter in mathematics, science, and logic. They also include the types of problems referred to as brainteasers, which have been made popular by Martin Gardner (1978, 1982). Below are two problems that would be considered academic problems in the Dimensions of Learning model. (The answers to these problems are at the end of this chapter on p. 152.)

Problem #1

> Bob says to Jana, "I gave away half of my rock collection and half of a rock to Louie. Then I gave half of what was left and half a rock more to Joe. I was left with one rock. How many rocks did I start with?"

Problem #2

> Ian starts up the mountain trail at 7:00 a.m. on Monday. He keeps walking at a steady pace and arrives at the top that night. He stays the night and starts back down the next morning at 7:00 a.m. This time he walks down the same trail at different speeds, sometimes walking very quickly, other times very slowly. He even stops to look at the scenery. He arrives back where he started at 3:00 p.m. on Tuesday. That night Ian runs into Devon, who tells him, "You know Ian, coming down the mountain you passed a spot at exactly the same time you passed it going up the mountain." Ian says, "No way! Coming down the mountain I walked at different speeds." But Devon was right. Explain why.

Academic problems like these have at least three characteristics that make them useful tools for reinforcing the habits of mind related to critical and creative thinking:

1. They are inherently engaging. One characteristic of academic problems is that they tend to "hook" people. Did you find yourself somewhat compelled to solve the sample problems after reading them? Did you turn to the end of the chapter to check the answers before continuing your reading? The human mind has a low tolerance for unanswered questions. Psychologists explain this phenomenon in terms of "closure." The concept of closure was used by Ebbinghaus as far back as 1897 to explain why human beings naturally fill in missing information. In 1953 Taylor used this principle to develop a "cloze test" to measure the readability of passages. Later, John Bormuth (1968) popularized the process in the field of reading diagnosis. The "cloze" test used in reading presents students with passages from which words have been systematically deleted. As students read these passages, the natural cognitive tendency to make sense of incomplete information quite literally compels them to fill in missing words. To illustrate, read the following sentence:

He went to the _____ and bought a loaf of _____.

It is difficult, if not impossible, to read this sentence without mentally filling in the words *store* and *bread,* respectively. Our cognitive system is designed to make sense of incomplete information. The same system drives us to solve problems like those above, which are incomplete in that they are, at least on the surface, missing a plausible explanation. How can you give away half a rock? Why do you have to pass at least one spot on the way down the hill at the same time that you passed it on the way up? Because academic questions are cognitively incomplete, then, they are naturally motivating. Even students who say they don't like to solve them are usually compelled to at least try. For this reason, such problems are inherently engaging.

2. They are easily placed in the curriculum. Hunter (1976) has popularized the notion of "sponge activities," or "learning opportunities which sop up those precious moments of waiting time which otherwise would be lost" (Hunter 1976, p. 76). She says that sponge activities are to be used "whenever there is an unavoidable waiting period before a planned activity can start, or when students finish an assignment and have some time left over." I have seen teachers in grades K–12 use problems like the ones above to this end. For example, one middle school social studies teacher had a ready store of academic problems. Each day, the teacher would duplicate several of these problems. As students completed assignments or waited for class to begin, they would try to solve the two or three "problems of the day." Students usually approached the activity with enthusiasm, and as students were trying to solve the problems, the teacher would reinforce such dispositions as seeking accuracy and persevering even when answers and solutions are not immediately apparent.

Teachers can also use academic problems as "interactive bulletin boards." Suzanne Lochran, the principal at Pioneer Elementary School who has all of her students set academic and personal goals at the beginning of the year, also has large bulletin boards in the school hallways covered with problems like those in Figure 6.3. Different corridors throughout the school are dedicated to different types of problems, and problem types are changed on a regular basis. Each board has a pocket containing answers to the problems. As students pass through the hallways, they are encouraged to solve the various types of problems and then check their answers.

Using academic problems as sponge activities to promote reasoning is in keeping with the new standards of the National Council for the Teaching of Mathematics (NCTM). Specifically, NCTM (1989) has recommended that problem solving be used as a regular classroom activity to enhance students' reasoning ability and understanding of basic mathematical concepts. I would go even further and suggest that academic problem solving should permeate the school day in K–12 classrooms.

3. They are cognitively challenging. Rowe (1985) and others have shown that academic problem solving is one of the most complex of cognitive actions. Even the simplest of problems necessitates the use of such strategies as generating and testing hypotheses, trial and error, working backward, and considering alternative hypotheses. Given its complexity, academic problem solving demands the use of one or more of the mental habits of critical and creative thinking. I frequently use the following problem to illustrate that an academic problem can challenge all levels of intellectual ability. Unless you have heard it before, the problem will take you a few minutes to solve. Even if you read the answer at the back of the chapter, you'll still need to take some time to figure out the logic behind it. In short, this problem will challenge you intellectually and probably require your use of the mental habit of persevering even when answers and solutions are not immediately apparent. Take a few minutes to solve the problem before reading further.

Problem #3

> Three men were in prison. One was blind, another could see out of only one eye, and the third could see out of both eyes. The jailer told the three that he had five hats—three white and two red. He put a hat on each of the prisoners without allowing them to see the color

FIGURE 6.3
Academic Problems from an Interactive Bulletin Board

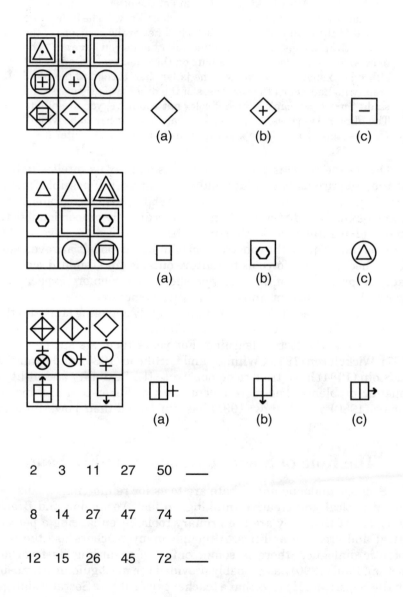

2   3   11   27   50   ___

8   14   27   47   74   ___

12   15   26   45   72   ___

❖

of their own hat. The jailer hid the remaining two hats so the prisoners could not see what color they were. The jailer then said, "If you can guess the color of your hat I will let you go free." He then asked the man who could see out of both eyes, "What color hat do you have on?" After looking at the hats of the other two prisoners, the man with sight in both eyes said: "I don't know." The jailer then turned to the man with one eye (who had heard the response of the man with both eyes) and said, "What color hat do you have on?" The man with one eye looked at the hats on the other two prisoners but still had to say: "I don't know." The jailer then turned to the blind man (who had heard the responses of the other two prisoners) and said, "Surely you can't tell what color hat you have, you are blind." The blind prisoner said, "Of course, I can. My hat has to be white." He was right. How did he know that his hat had to be white?

One of the reasons problems like this one tax us intellectually is that they require us to consider and test a number of possible "mental models." In fact, Johnson-Laird (1975, 1983, 1985) has dramatically illustrated that the difficulty of a problem is directly proportional to the number of mental models that must be considered to solve it. And problems that require the construction of unusual models are even more difficult because they force us to venture outside our standard schemas. Academic problems not only tax our short-term memory capacity but also require us to invent unusual cognitive structures.

In summary, academic problems are highly engaging activities that fit easily into the curriculum and are challenging enough to elicit the mental habits of effective learning. For years theorists such as Polya (1957), Wickelgren (1975), Whimby and Lochhead (1985), and Bransford and Stein (1984) have tried to demonstrate the flexibility and utility of academic problems. The more recent work of Feuerstein and his colleagues (1980) and Pogrow (1991) has illustrated their powerful effect on academic learning.

The Role of Socratic Dialogue and Debate

Socratic dialogue and debate are tools for reinforcing the dispositions of critical and creative thinking. In fact, Vosniadou and Brewer (1987) assert that they are the primary tools for enhancing a person's critical and creative abilities. Although many teachers use the term "Socratic dialogue," there is some confusion regarding its form and function. Paul (1990) has probably provided the most guidance for using it in the classroom. He says that a teacher can facilitate Socratic dialogue by asking five types of questions as students discuss specific topics:

• Questions of clarification: For example, "What do you mean by . . ? Could you give me an example?"

• Questions that probe assumptions: For example, "What are you assuming? What is underlying what you say?"

• Questions that probe reasons and evidence: For example, "How do you know? What are your reasons for saying that?"

• Questions about viewpoints on perspectives: For example, "What might someone say who believed that . . . ? What is an alternative?"

• Questions that probe implications and consequences: For example, "What are you implying by that? Because of that what might happen?"

Ideally, of course, students should learn to ask these questions themselves as they participate in discussions. Teachers can help them learn to do so by providing guided practice in the form of organized activities:

• Conduct an initial exploratory discussion about a complex issue and help students break the issue into simpler parts. Students can then choose the aspects they want to explore and focus their discussion on these more specific aspects of the issue.

• Set up a "fishbowl" discussion. One-third of the class sits in a circle and discusses a topic. The rest of the class, in a circle around the others, listens and takes notes, then discusses the discussion.

Debate is closely related to Socratic dialogue. Here students prepare and defend an argument for one side of an issue. I once listened to junior high students debate the ban of fur sales, artfully using Socratic questions to argue their cases. I was impressed by their level of expertise. Apparently, such skills are common in Greensboro, North Carolina, where the local school district has systematically implemented Richard Paul's theories (Williamson 1990).

Don't Underestimate Primary Students

At times, when presented with the notion of teaching and reinforcing productive habits of mind, some primary teachers have asserted that such habits are too abstract for primary students to grasp. Unfortunately, this is a common misconception. All students, even those in the primary grades, can and do use the mental habits of self-regulation, critical thinking, and creative thinking. Several studies have shown that young children function at a much higher level than previously thought, as long as the content they are dealing with is familiar to them (in Yussen 1985).

Debra Pickering, one of the co-authors of the Dimensions of Learning program, told me a story about a 1st grade class in which the teacher was reinforcing the mental habits of restraining impulsivity and being open-minded. Students were asked to identify explicit examples in their own lives and in others'. At first, the teacher wondered if students really understood the concept. Her answer came when students were asked to say good-bye to the student teacher. One student presented the student teacher with the "Happy-Gram" in Figure 6.4.

FIGURE 6.4
A Happy-Gram

In case you cannot decipher the student's handwriting and spelling, his message reads: "Mrs. McD, she's done a great job teaching and restraining impulsivity and being open minded. Great job!" When asked to explain what he meant by his remarks, the student was able to identify specific examples of how the student teacher had restrained impulsivity and remained open-minded. As this example shows, even young students can understand the mental habits of self-regulation, critical thinking, and creative thinking. It would be a serious mistake to delay teaching and reinforcing the habits of mind because of a misconception about the abilities and interests of younger students.

Planning for Uses of the Habits of Mind

As with the other four dimensions, the habits of mind require planning and overt attention if students are to value, learn, and practice them. To explore this idea, let's consider Ms. Conklin's planning for Dimension 5.

Ms. Conklin's Planning for Dimension 5

Throughout her career, Ms. Conklin has assumed that she has been reinforcing positive habits of mind. Only recently has she begun to overtly teach them. Her motivation for planning in a more overt manner increased when she realized that she could not remember the last time she did anything specifically to reinforce a productive habit of mind. She thought to herself, "They're just like attitudes and perceptions. I think I do things to reinforce them, but I'm not really sure I actually do."

Since then, she has planned to reinforce a few of the habits of mind during each unit. In the last unit, she emphasized planning and seeking accuracy. In this unit, she decides to emphasize three mental habits: one creative-thinking habit and two self-regulatory habits:

- Engaging intensely in tasks even when answers and solutions are not immediately apparent (creative).
- Becoming aware of your own thinking (self-regulatory).
- Using resources (self-regulatory).

She decides that she will introduce the critical-thinking habit by telling students the story of how she took seven years to get her master's degree, transferring to two universities and, at times, feeling that she would never finish. She concludes that she will not introduce the self-regulatory mental habits because she and the students have discussed them before.

To reinforce the creative-thinking habit, she decides to use problem solving as a sponge activity. Each day she'll select a few problems and use them when class slows down, when students' energy starts to wane. She will foster the mental habit of using available resources by reminding students about its importance as they work on their projects. She will also ask students a few "probing" questions so that they can reflect on their use of all the mental habits being emphasized in the unit. As she makes these decisions, she records them in a planning guide (see Figure 6.5).

Ms. Conklin's planning illustrates three basic decisions:

1. Which mental habits will be emphasized? It would be impractical to focus on all fifteen of the mental habits listed in this chapter in a single unit of instruction. A teacher can legitimately emphasize only one or two in any one- to six-week period of time. In her unit, Ms. Conklin focuses on three mental habits. The ideal, though, is that over time students will be exposed to all the mental habits in direct and indirect ways. When presenting this notion to teachers, I commonly ask, "What would education be like if the productive habits of mind were reinforced to some extent in every unit of instruction?" Although the answer to this question is pure conjecture, we can suggest some interesting possibilities. For instance, perhaps these fifteen mental habits are the "core curriculum" that ties all subjects together, the one set of skills that do transfer to almost all learning situations.

2. Which mental habits will be introduced? As I noted earlier in this chapter, given their lack of emphasis in our society, many of the mental habits must be introduced to students so that their nature and importance are clear. This, of course, takes time away from content coverage. Once introduced, however, the mental habits can be easily integrated into a unit of instruction. Ms. Conklin decided that only the creative-thinking habit would require introduction. The two self-regulatory habits had already been discussed at an earlier date.

3. How will the mental habits be reinforced? Introducing a mental habit without reinforcing it does little to help students internalize it and make it part of their regular behavior. Consequently, from the Dimensions of Learning perspective, activities that reinforce selected habits of mind should be as common as activities that deal with content. The activities Ms. Conklin selected will certainly take some time—but not an excessive amount. In many cases, then, the habits of mind can easily be part of regular classroom instruction without sacrificing content. Indeed, teachers who systematically teach and reinforce the productive habits of mind report that it is well worth the effort because, once learned, the habits are powerful tools for increasing the effectiveness of students' learning.

FIGURE 6.5
Unit Planning Guide for
Dimension 5: Productive Habits of Mind

What I will do to help students engage in:

Self-Regulated Thinking:	Critical Thinking:	Creative Thinking:
✓ Help students become aware of their own thinking	✓ Encourage students to be accurate and seek accuracy	— Encourage students to engage intensely in tasks even when answers/solutions are not immediately apparent
✓ Encourage students to plan	— Encourage students to be clear and seek clarity	— Encourage students to push the limits of their knowledge and abilities
— Encourage students to use resources	— Encourage students to be open-minded	— Encourage students to generate and maintain their own standards
— Encourage students to be sensitive to feedback	— Encourage students to restrain impulsivity	— Encourage students to generate new ways of viewing things
— Encourage students to evaluate their actions	— Encourage students to take a position and defend it when the situation warrants it	
	— Encourage students to be sensitive to others	

Activities:

Self-Regulated Thinking Activities:
- I will encourage students to identify resources
- I will include 2 probes dealing with awareness of thinking:
  (1) "What do you notice about how you think?"
  (2) "When did you notice that others were thinking about their own thinking?"

Critical Thinking Activities:
- I will include 2 probes in learning log:
  (1) "What evidence do you have that you stick to a task when it is difficult."
  (2) When did you want to 'give up' during this unit?
- I will have "problems of the day"

Creative Thinking Activities:

❖ ❖ ❖

In summary, the productive habits of mind emphasized in Dimension 5 are similar to the positive attitudes and perceptions highlighted in Dimension 1: they permeate everything that occurs in the classroom. When students use productive habits of mind, they enhance their learning; when they don't, they impede their learning.

Answers to Problems

Problem #1: Bob started with 7 rocks. He gave Louise half of the collection (3½) plus half a rock. That means he gave Louie 4 and had 3 left. Of the remaining three, he gave Joe half of the collection (1½) plus half a rock. Thus he gave 2 away and had one left.

Problem #2: Given that Ian started and ended at the same time on both days, he had to be at the same spot at the same time once on both days, even though he was traveling at different rates. The best way to prove this to yourself is to imagine Ian as two people. One starts up the mountain at 7:00 a.m. and the other starts down the mountain at the same time. If they both reach their destination at 3:00 p.m., they will have to cross at some point on the path even though they traveled at different rates.

Problem #3: Given that the man with two good eyes and the man with one good eye could not figure out the color of their hats, the blind man had to be wearing a white hat for the following reasons: Because the man with two good eyes couldn't figure out the color of his hat, he must have seen a white and a white or a white and a red (if he had seen two red hats he would have known the color of his hat). Hearing the answer of the man with two good eyes, the man with one good eye must have seen a white hat on the blind man. If he had seen a red hat on the blind man he could have concluded that his hat had to be white because he would have known that the man with two good eyes also saw the red hat on the blind man. The reasoning of the man with one good eye would have been: "If the man with two good eyes saw a red hat on the blind man like I am seeing and couldn't figure out the color of his hat, then he must have seen a white hat on me." Thus, if the blind man had a red hat on, at least the man with one good eye (the second prisoner to guess) would have been able to figure out the color of his hat. Consequently, the blind man must have had a white hat because that is the only way one of the first two prisoners could not have figured out the color of his own hat.

7

❖

Putting It All Together

❖

As the previous chapters have illustrated, each of the five dimensions requires teachers to make important decisions. But how do teachers structure these decisions so they work together in an integrated way? And how do teachers relate the dimensions to other innovations and issues in education, such as cooperative learning, writing across the curriculum, and assessment? In short, how do teachers use the dimensions to organize instruction?

At a very basic level, planning a unit using the Dimensions of Learning framework is a matter of asking five sets of questions, each of which has already been discussed in the previous chapters. These questions are summarized in Figure 7.1. It is important to realize that the order in which these questions are presented does not necessarily represent the order in which teachers attend to them when planning a unit of instruction. In fact, during the development of the Dimensions of Learning framework, the developers found that teachers familiar with the framework use one of three basic planning models.

The Dimensions Planning Models

The three Dimensions planning models have in common one primary characteristic—namely, the manner in which Dimensions 1 and 5 are considered. Most teachers using the Dimensions of Learning framework tend to deal with Dimension 1 (positive attitudes and perceptions about learning) and Dimension 5 (productive habits of mind) as "background considerations" that to some extent are independent of content (i.e., Dimensions 2, 3, and 4). In other words, positive attitudes and perceptions and productive habits of mind are learning goals in any unit

FIGURE 7.1
Questions to Answer When Planning a Unit

Dimension 1

1. What will be done to help students develop positive attitudes and perceptions about the learning climate?

   a. What will be done to help students feel accepted by the teacher and their peers?
   b. What will be done to help students perceive the classroom as a comfortable and orderly place?

2. What will be done to help students develop positive attitudes and perceptions about classroom tasks?

   a. What will be done to help students perceive classroom tasks as valuable?
   b. What will be done to help students believe they can perform classroom tasks?
   c. What will be done to help students understand and be clear about classroom tasks?

Dimension 2

Declarative Knowledge:

   1. What are the general topics?
   2. What are the specifics?
   3. How will students experience the information?
   4. How will students be aided in constructing meaning?
   5. How will students be aided in organizing the information?
   6. How will students be aided in storing the information?

Procedural Knowledge:

   1. What skills and processes do students really need to master?
   2. How will students be aided in constructing models?
   3. How will students be aided in shaping the skill or process?
   4. How will students be aided in internalizing the skill or process?

(continued)

FIGURE 7.1
Questions to Answer When Planning a Unit
(continued)

Dimension 3

1. What information will be extended and refined?
2. What activities will be used to help students extend and refine knowledge?

Dimension 4

1. What are the big issues?
2. How many issues will be considered?
3. Who will structure the tasks?
4. What types of products will students create?
5. To what extent will students work in cooperative groups?

Dimension 5

1. Which mental habits will be emphasized?
2. Which mental habits will be introduced?
3. How will the mental habits be reinforced?

of instruction in any content area at any grade level. They are the environment in which content instruction occurs, and thus, teachers usually make decisions about these two dimensions *after* they have planned for Dimensions 2, 3, and 4. In short, these two dimensions are viewed as a set, and decisions about them are complementary to, but separate from, decisions about content. It is the manner in which teachers make decisions about Dimensions 2, 3, and 4 that distinguishes the three planning models.

Model 1: Focus on Knowledge

When using Model 1, the teacher focuses on Dimension 2, acquiring and integrating declarative and procedural knowledge. This means that specific concepts, principles, and skills are the focus of the unit. Everything that happens in the classroom "serves" these learning goals. Thus, the teacher selects extending and refining activities (Dimension 3) and meaningful-use tasks (Dimension 4) that will reinforce and deepen students' understanding of the declarative and procedural knowledge identified as the focus of the unit. The planning sequence for this model might be depicted as follows:

Step #1

Identify the declarative and procedural knowledge (Dimension 2) that will be the focus of the unit.

↓

Step #2

Select extending and refining activities that will reinforce and deepen students' understanding of the declarative and procedural knowledge identified in Step #1.

↓

Step #3

Select a meaningful-use task (Dimension 4) that will reinforce and deepen students' understanding of the declarative and procedural knowledge identified in Step #1.

Model 1 has these general characteristics:

• Concepts and principles (as opposed to discrete facts) tend to be the focus of a unit. Less frequently, a skill or content area procedure is the focus and, when it is, selected declarative knowledge is also featured.

• Extending and refining activities (Dimension 3) are usually emphasized more than meaningful-use tasks (Dimension 4).

• Usually, only one meaningful-use task is used in the unit and the teacher makes sure that students know the task is essential to helping them understand the knowledge identified in Step #1.

Model 2: Focus on Issues

When using this model, teachers focus on Dimension 4, the meaningful use of knowledge. Specifically, teachers identify an issue related to the general theme of the unit and decide what kind of meaningful-use task might be associated with the issue. For example, if there is an issue about how or why something happened, then historical investigation becomes the focus of the unit. If there is a phenomenon to be studied, then experimental inquiry becomes the focus, and so on. Once the issue and its related meaningful-use task are identified, the declarative and procedural knowledge (Dimension 2) and any extending and refining activities (Dimension 3) needed to complete the task are identified. Work in Dimensions 2 and 3 supports the meaningful-use task that has been selected. The decision-making process for Model 2 might be represented in this way:

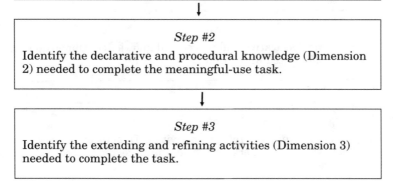

Step #1

Identify an important issue and its related meaningful-use task (Dimension 4).

Step #2

Identify the declarative and procedural knowledge (Dimension 2) needed to complete the meaningful-use task.

Step #3

Identify the extending and refining activities (Dimension 3) needed to complete the task.

Model 2 has these general characteristics:

• The unit contains only one meaningful-use task. In the primary grades, an extending and refining activity (Dimension 3) may be used instead because this kind of activity is usually more appropriate for young students.

• Acquiring and integrating declarative and procedural knowledge is a secondary goal in the unit.

• Extending and refining activities are frequently deemphasized (unless one is selected as the focus of the unit in the primary grades).

Model 3: Focus on Student Exploration

Model 3 most closely resembles the developers' original concept of the workings of the Dimensions of Learning framework. As in model 1, the teacher first identifies the declarative and procedural knowledge (Dimension 2) that will be highlighted in the unit. She also identifies the extending and refining activities (Dimension 3) that will reinforce that knowledge. In a departure from both models 1 and 2, however, the teacher does not identify a meaningful-use task (Dimension 4), but asks students to select their own tasks, or projects, for making meaningful use of knowledge. The teacher's job is to assist students in choosing a project. Although these projects will certainly be related to the declarative and procedural knowledge the teacher has identified, the teacher does not try to force a close fit, but encourages students to explore issues and interesting questions that arise naturally in the unit. In effect, students have the freedom to study issues that are beyond the scope of the declarative and procedural knowledge identified by the teacher. Using this model, the planning process might be depicted in the following way:

Step #1

Identify the declarative and procedural knowledge (Dimension 2) to be highlighted in the unit.

↓

Step #2

Identify extending and refining activities (Dimension 3) that will help students understand the declarative and procedural knowledge.

↓

Step #3

Identify ways to help students select meaningful-use tasks (Dimension 4).

Model 3 has these general characteristics:

• The types of meaningful-use tasks or projects undertaken by students are very diverse.

• A greater proportion of class time is devoted to these projects (Dimension 4) because students develop their own.

In choosing which of the Dimensions planning models to use, some teachers look at how well each model helps them achieve specified "outcomes."

How the Models Relate to Expected Outcomes

Many schools and districts are moving toward an outcome-based approach to schooling. As Spady (1988) notes, an obvious way to increase the probability that students will acquire the knowledge, skills, and attitudes necessary for success in the information age is to specify such "outcomes" (knowledge, skills, and attitudes) and orient curriculum, instruction, and assessment toward them:

> By designing our educational system to achieve clearly defined outcomes, we will free ourselves from the traditional rigidity of schools and increase the likelihood that all students will learn (Spady 1988, p. 4).

Although not formally a part of the outcome-based education (OBE) movement, the Dimensions of Learning model is very compatible with it. In fact, Spady frequently cites the Aurora Public Schools in Aurora, Colorado, as an example of OBE in action, and the Aurora Public Schools use Dimensions of Learning as one of their basic instructional programs.

In simple terms, an outcome is a clear statement of what a school or district expects a student to do or know when instruction is complete. From an outcome-based perspective, then, the initial test of how well a unit has been planned is the extent to which the teacher can answer the question "What are the expected outcomes of this unit?" Although all three planning models are fairly flexible in terms of the outcomes they can address, each lends itself more strongly to certain types than to others. Model 1 is suited to a more traditional approach, in which the expected outcome is a mastery of the knowledge and skills indigenous to specific content areas. Model 2 lends itself to outcomes that deal more with the application of knowledge to large issues or topics that are often interdisciplinary in nature. Finally, Model 3 lends itself to outcomes geared toward individualized learning and the enhancement of self-directed learning.

Regardless of the planning model used or the outcomes identified, the true artistry involved in using the Dimensions of Learning framework resides in the sequencing of learning activities. The diversity of instructional activities implicit in the Dimensions framework calls for a variety of instructional models, two of which are particularly suited to Dimensions, presentation classes and workshop classes.

The Dance Between Presentation and Workshop Classes

A successful unit of instruction can be seen as a dance between two types of classes: presentation classes, where the teacher charts the direction of learning, and workshop classes, where students have more control over their learning.

Presentation Classes

Presentation classes are geared toward helping students acquire and integrate new knowledge (Dimension 2) and extend and refine that knowledge (Dimension 3). It is important that presentation classes not be associated with a didactic approach to instruction. Although the focus of learning in this kind of class is directed by the teacher, the act of learning is still highly constructive and learner-centered. If you review some of the instructional activities described in Chapter 3, you'll see that the techniques for helping students construct, organize, and store knowledge assume that students must initially construct meaning using their prior knowledge. Students must arrange information in ways that are personally relevant, and elaborate on information in personal and meaningful ways. Similarly, the techniques for helping students build models and shape and internalize procedural knowledge force the learner to use prior knowledge to acquire and integrate this new information. The techniques used to help students extend and refine their knowledge, as described in Chapter 4, are also highly constructive in nature. Curricular focus and teacher direction, then, do not necessarily imply didactic instruction.

A typical presentation class has some, but not all, of the characteristics of the methodologies described by Hunter (1984) and Rosenshine (1983, 1986). For example, a presentation class usually begins with some type of anticipatory set: an activity that helps students develop interest in the learning experience. Similarly, a presentation class commonly ends with some type of closure activity in which students summarize what they have learned.

Additionally, regardless of what type of information is emphasized (declarative or procedural) or what phase of learning is addressed, presentation classes involve some clear modeling of the processes involved. For example, if the focus of the presentation class were on organizing information from a field trip, the teacher might demonstrate the use of a particular graphic organizer. In short, presentation classes commonly include activities that perform the following functions:

- Help stimulate interest in the topic
- Relate new information to existing information
- Provide clear goals and directions
- Demonstrate or model important activities
- Provide closure

These five functions do not have to be part of every presentation class, nor do they have to be performed in a set order. Over the course of a unit, however, they should be systematically addressed.

Workshop Classes

The workshop approach is firmly established within what might be loosely called the "writing process" and the "whole-language" movements. Atwell (1987) and Hansen (1987) have detailed the uses of writing and reading workshops across a variety of grade levels. What has not been well articulated, though, is how the workshop approach can be used with processes other than reading and writing: processes such as decision making, investigation, experimental inquiry, problem solving, and invention used across various content domains.

The structure of the workshop approach makes it an ideal tool for facilitating the more student-directed activity of using knowledge in meaningful ways (Dimension 4). Generally, a workshop class has three parts: a mini-lesson, an activity period, and a sharing period. Each of the components of the workshop has a specific function.

The mini-lesson. As its name implies, the mini-lesson is short (five to ten minutes). For the most part, it is a time for the teacher to provide guidance and assistance as students work on projects (i.e., tasks that require them to use knowledge meaningfully). At first a teacher might use the mini-lesson to help students select or construct their projects. Recall that Ms. Conklin planned to give students a choice of two projects for the unit on weather. She also planned to encourage students to create their own projects, using mini-lessons in the first few workshops to model how to construct an invention task and an experimental task using information from the unit.

Once students have selected or constructed their own projects, the mini-lesson is used to provide students with resources. For example, Ms. Conklin planned to use the succeeding mini-lessons to present various strategies of hypothesis testing for students' experimental inquiry projects, and to guide students to resources they could use in their invention projects. The mini-lesson, then, is a vehicle for teachers' direct input into student projects.

The activity period. An activity period is a block of time (twenty to forty-five minutes) in which students work individually, in pairs, or in small groups on their projects. For example, during an activity period in Ms. Conklin's class, one or two small groups of students might be involved in the invention task she has suggested while other students work independently on their own invention projects. Other groups might work cooperatively on experimental inquiry projects while still other students conduct individual experimental inquiry projects.

While students work on their projects, the teacher's main function is to "conference" with individual students. Conferencing (described in detail in a subsequent section) is at the heart of the workshop approach, because it allows the teacher to establish a relationship of coach and coworker with students that is difficult (perhaps impossible) to establish in presentation classes. Presentation classes are meant to focus on rather specific learning objectives that require a good deal of teacher orchestration, whereas workshop classes are devoted to student projects, which by definition require the teacher to turn over control to the students. This doesn't mean that students are set adrift. Rather, the teacher now functions as coach, pointing out possible pitfalls, steering each student toward useful resources and, quite frequently, puzzling with a student over some sticky problem that has arisen within a project. Of course, in this new arrangement student and teacher need time to interact on a one-to-one basis, a requirement that is fulfilled by conferencing.

If conferences are kept short (five to ten minutes per student), a teacher can move efficiently through the class. For example, assuming workshop activity periods last an average of twenty-five minutes and conferences an average of five minutes, during each workshop a teacher can meet with five students. Assuming that there are thirty students in a class, a teacher can meet with each student every six workshops. Of course, a teacher can see more students in a workshop by reducing the amount of time for each conference or by increasing the amount of time for the activity period. And if students are working on a project as a cooperative group, a teacher might meet with the entire group, thus significantly decreasing the average per pupil conference time.

The sharing period. The sharing period of a workshop is quite short, usually only five to ten minutes. During this time, students discuss a variety of topics, ranging from insights to problems to strategies. For example, one student might describe how his awareness of a topic has grown as a result of his invention task. Another student might describe a problem he is having on his project and ask for help. And another might describe a new way she has found to test hypotheses in experimental inquiry tasks. The hallmark of sharing period is that the students and teacher freely discuss their learning as students work on their projects.

Figure 7.2 shows one way of conceptualizing the three parts of a workshop class.

LEARNING LOGS IN THE WORKSHOP

The workshop approach, particularly the act of conferencing, is greatly enhanced if students are encouraged to use learning logs. A learning log as described in this model might be considered a type of journal. Atwell (1987), Calkins (1986), and Macrorie (1984) have described the use of journals in the classroom. A learning log is usually nothing more than a spiral notebook in which students record a variety of types of responses. These responses serve several purposes:

• Allowing students to express thoughts and ideas they would otherwise not get to express.
• Providing students and the teacher with a record of student thinking throughout a project.
• Providing students and the teacher with an arena for dialogue about the habits of mind.
• Providing students and teacher with an arena for dialogue about content.

To ensure a variety of responses, teachers should ask students to make two basic types of responses in their learning logs, free responses and structured responses.

FIGURE 7.2
A Workshop Class

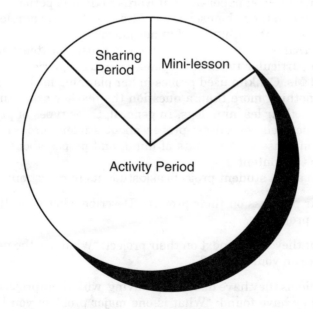

Free responses are just that: responses in which students are asked to record anything that seems important to them. This type of response can be likened to what is referred to as an "expressive" response. Drawing on Sapir's (1921) notion of "expressive speech," Briton and his colleagues (Britton, Burgess, Martin, McLeod, and Rosen 1975) coined the term expressive writing. They state that expressive writing is "self-expressive" or "close to the self." It "reveals the speaker, verbalizing his consciousness" (p. 90). Discussing the importance of expressive writing and the extent to which it was found in a major study, Toby Fulwiler notes:

> Expressive writing often looks like speech written down and is usually characterized by first-person pronouns, informal style and colloquial diction. [In a large scale study of the types of writing done in secondary schools] it accounted for 5.5% of the total sample collected, with no evidence of its use outside of English classes (Fulwiler 1986, p. 24).

Fulwiler goes on to say that the low percentage of expressive writing in the English classroom and its total absence in other classes attests to the lack of importance given to student self-expression and student self-inquiry that are at the core of effective learning.

Free response writing, then, encourages students to put whatever thoughts they wish on paper—to put words to their experiences so they can better understand themselves. Figure 7.3 shows examples of free responses a student might record in her journal.

Structured responses are so called because the teacher guides students to particular types of responses through queries or "probes." (Recall that Ms. Conklin used probes in her planning for Dimension 5.) A probe is nothing more than a question the teacher asks students to respond to in their learning logs. In general, three types of probes are used in structured responses: probes about student projects, probes about students' use of the habits of mind, and probes about students' progress on the content.

Probes about student projects ask students to report on:

• Their progress on their project: "Describe where you think you are in your project."

• What they will do next on their project: "What are the next steps you will take on your project?"

• Problems they have had, or are having, with their project and the solutions they have found: "What is one major problem you have had with your project and how did you solve it?" or "What is one major problem you are having with your project and how do you plan to solve it?"

• Conclusions they have reached about themselves or the content as a result of the project: "What is one major insight you have had about the content as a result of your project?" or "What is one major insight you have had about yourself as a result of your project?"

Probes about students' use of the habits of mind ask students to:

• Describe specific situations in which they have used or could have used one or more of the habits of mind: "Describe how you have used or could have used the critical-thinking habit of mind of seeking accuracy."

FIGURE 7.3
Student's Free-Response Journal Entry

Tuesday
The guest lecturer made sense to me. I think I understand air pressure now and how it relates to weather.

Wednesday
I didn't like today at all — the activity made no sense and I really didn't care about it.

Friday
This project looks like it will be tough. I'm going to need help.

• Evaluate their use of one or more of the habits of mind: "Evaluate how well you have been doing on the self-regulatory mental habit of planning."

• Describe how they plan to use one or more of the habits of mind: "Describe how you will be using the creative-thinking mental habit of seeing things in new and unusual ways."

Probes about content ask students to do the following:

• Describe their confusions about the content: "What are some of the things you have been confused about in class?"

• Describe their confidence in their knowledge: "How do you feel about what we're learning? Do you think you're doing well?"

To explore how these probes might be used, consider Ms. Conklin's weather unit. On Monday of a given week, Ms. Conklin might ask students to make a free response in their learning logs simply by saying, "This is free response time; please write something in your logs." On Tuesday, she might orchestrate a structured response about student projects by asking, "What's the biggest problem you are having right now in your project?" On Wednesday, she might use a probe that elicits a response about students' use and understanding of one of the habits of mind that are the focus of the unit: "Explain what you have been doing to use resources more effectively." Finally, on Thursday she might use a probe dealing with content: "What are you most confused about so far?"

To interpret student journals, Ms. Conklin would keep a record of the types of responses students made and the exact probe questions that she used:

> • *Monday* free response
> • *Tuesday* probe about projects: "What is the biggest problem you are having?"
> • *Wednesday* probe about habit of mind: "Explain what you have been doing to use resources more effectively."
> • *Thursday* probe about content: "What are you most confused about so far?"

With this record, Ms. Conklin would be well equipped to confer with students.

PORTFOLIOS IN THE WORKSHOP

Portfolios are another type of record that fits well in the workshop approach. Their utility in language arts classes has been widely praised (Tierney, Carter, and Desai 1991; Goodman, Goodman, and Wood 1989;

❖

Harp 1991). Their use in classes that are not focused on the writing process is not so well documented. In the Dimensions of Learning model, portfolios are basically repositories for students' finished and unfinished work:

- The products of completed projects
- Artifacts
- Incomplete projects
- Tests
- Ideas for new projects

For example, a student might put his audiotaped report for a specific project in his portfolio along with two tests on which he performed particularly well. He might also include a poem written to represent an aesthetic experience associated with a project. Finally, he might keep a list of projects that he'd like to do. Portfolios encompass more than a single unit's work; they represent student achievement across units and, ideally, across content areas. Portfolios are now being used as an alternative method of assessment, primarily in writing instruction. From the Dimensions of Learning perspective, they can be used as powerful evaluative tools across all content areas.

CONFERENCING IN THE WORKSHOP

For the most part, while students are working on projects during the activity period of a workshop class, the teacher is conferencing with individual students or groups of students. As stated earlier, conferencing is the heart of the workshop approach because it allows for the one-to-one interaction between student and teacher that can drastically change the role of both. Although every conference has one basic function—to establish a line of communication between teacher and student—it is useful to think about three different focuses that might be used: habits of mind, projects, and content.

Habits of Mind Focus. When the focus is on habits of mind, the purpose of the conference is to reinforce the use and development of the mental habits of self-regulation, critical thought, and creative thought. The materials and information emphasized in this type of conference are the sections of the learning logs in which students have recorded free responses that may touch on the habits of mind, and structured responses that relate directly to the habits of mind. In this conference, the teacher and student interact in three ways:

- The teacher notes positive instances of the student's use of the habits of mind.

- The teacher notes negative instances of the student's use of the habits of mind.
- The teacher and student develop strategies for working on specific habits of mind.

For example, Ms. Conklin might say, "Mary, I've noticed that you're really trying to be accurate lately, particularly when you. . . ." She might also comment on Mary's not using the mental habits: "I think you missed an opportunity the other day, though, to use the mental habit of being precise when you were. . . ."

Besides noting how students have used or not used the habits of mind, the teacher can also help students create plans for increasing their proficiency in using a specific mental habit. For example, if a student says she wants to improve her use of one (or more) of the habits of creative thinking (e.g., engaging intensely in tasks even when answers or solutions are not apparent), the teacher might suggest specific situations in which the mental habit might be most useful (e.g., while studying for a particularly difficult test) and specific strategies that could be used to enhance the disposition (e.g., when you find yourself getting frustrated, stop working for a while and try to refresh yourself; when your energy picks up, then return to your studies). After establishing an action plan for a specific mental habit, the teacher and student might set a date for another conference in which to consider the progress made on the goal.

Project Focus. When a conference focuses on projects, its purpose is to provide guidance for students' work on their projects, thus the conference naturally revolves around the sections of the learning logs in which students have written free responses about their projects and structured responses to probes from the teacher about their projects. The teacher and student discuss progress on the project and any problems the student might be having. Then they jointly plan next steps for the project. For example, a student might describe her difficulty in setting up an experiment to test her hypothesis for an experimental inquiry project. The teacher would then help the student devise an appropriate experiment. The conference is also used to provide guidance about what resources are necessary to complete the project. The teacher might point the student to a particular book or person who can help her with the next phase of the project. Within the framework of the conference, teacher and student become partners in pursuit of a shared goal.

Content Focus. The purpose of a conference with a content focus is for the teacher and student to talk about content in a nonthreatening, nonevaluative way. What's important here are responses to content probes in student learning logs. Using this information, a teacher and a student might discuss any confusions or concerns the student has. For example, based on an excerpt in the student's learning log, Ms. Conklin might say, "Juanita, you say in your learning log that you're having trouble understanding the concept of air pressure. How can I help you out?"

Given the limited amount of time a teacher has to meet with students, it is unrealistic to expect that an entire conference will be devoted to the habits of mind, projects, or content. Rather, within a single conference a teacher might have two or three focuses. When these shifts in emphasis are made, however, the teacher should communicate them to students so that the purpose of the interaction is clear to both teacher and student.

The Role of Reciprocity. The habits of mind conference, the project conference, and the content conference are all highly personal experiences. To be fully successful, they require openness and personal disclosure not only from students but also from teachers. I recommend that teachers also keep a learning log. Then, during habits of mind conferences, the teacher can share insights about herself and about her progress in cultivating a particular habit of mind (e.g., "I notice that you've been trying to improve your ability to hang in there when you can't find an answer or solution. I've been working on the same mental habit. Let me tell you what I've noticed about my behavior. . . ."). This reciprocity of openness and disclosure can help change the traditional relationship between teachers and students. Atwell (1987) asserts that it is reciprocity that breaks down the current ineffective learning structure in which the teacher is viewed as the presenter of information and students as the receivers of information.

Choreographing the Dance

It is important that presentation classes and workshop classes support each other. Specifically, it is important that in any unit of instruction the presentation and workshop classes be staggered. Figure 7.4 shows Ms. Conklin's arrangement of presentation and workshop classes for the weather unit. Ms. Conklin has decided to have nine workshop classes over four weeks' time. (Note that one workshop will last only a half-period.) Most of the presentation classes occur at the beginning of the unit, and workshop classes become more frequent as the unit progresses. This is because students need a certain amount of information before they can effectively direct their own projects. Over time, the emphasis in a unit of instruction gradually shifts to the use of

FIGURE 7.4
Arrangement of Classes for the Weather Unit

	Monday	Tuesday	Wednesday	Thursday	Friday
Week #1	(P) textbook pp. 15-18 on barometer and thermometer	(P) Channel 9 guest lecturer on rise/drop in air pressure	(P) abstracting activity on air pressure	(P) filmstrip on barometer and thermom.	(W) • present steps in experimental inquiry • students develop projects
Week #2	(P) construct model for process of reading barometer; students make flowchart	(W) present resources for projects	(W) students work on projects; I conference	(P) shape process of reading barometer; textbook pp 21-23 on tornado	(P) • students practice reading barometer • compare tornado and hurricane
Week #3	(P) • field trip to university • induction activity on bus home (finish for homework.)	(W) students work on projects; I conference	(W) students work on projects; I conference	(P) • students practice reading barometer • read "Weather and War"	(P) film: "Partly Cloudy, Cold, and Humid"
Week #4	(W) students work on projects; I conference	(W) students work on projects; I conference	(P) students practice reading barometer (W) students work on projects; I conference	(W) students work on projects; I conference	(P) class collage

(P) = Presentation Class

(W) = Workshop Class

170

knowledge. Staggering presentation and workshop classes maximizes the opportunities for providing guidance and direction for student projects and reduces the likelihood of boredom.

Assessing the Dimensions of Learning

No instructional model would be complete without thoroughly addressing the issue of assessment, in terms of both what is assessed and how it is assessed. A growing body of research indicates that assessment drives instruction, which in turn drives learning (Frederiksen and Collins 1989). For example, in a study of academic learning in the United States, Doyle (1983) concluded that students learn best what is assessed. Shepard (1989) echoes that the nature of tests and the import given to them causes educators to adjust instruction to fit the test: after reviewing the research in the testing field, she concluded that there is ample evidence to validate the principle that testing shapes instruction.

In and of itself, the tendency of testing to shape instruction and learning is not negative. It is the type of testing that is most heavily weighted and commonly used in education, namely standardized tests, that is worrisome. Standardized tests generally measure mental abilities that have been referred to as "lower order" in nature. In the Dimensions of Learning terminology, they tend to measure students' ability to acquire and integrate information, not to extend and refine it or to use it meaningfully. In a series of studies conducted on two standardized test batteries, my colleagues and I found that the tests focused on the ability to recall and recognize factual information, not on the ability to use or apply knowledge (Marzano and Costa 1988, Marzano and Jesse 1987). Similar conclusions have been reported by many others (Carey and Shavelson 1989, Frederiksen and Collins 1989, Shepard 1989).

If we expect students to honor the five dimensions of learning, we must assess students' use of the dimensions—or at the very least, comment on their use. The specifics of how each dimension can be assessed are addressed in depth in the *Dimensions of Learning Teacher's Manual*. Briefly, though, a teacher might use all of these types of information to assess the five dimensions:

- Direct observation of student behavior
- Regular classroom tests
- Student self-reports
- Free responses and answers to probes in learning logs
- Products of students' long-term projects

Deciding which of the dimensions of learning to concentrate assessment on is a major decision the teacher must make. Those of us who developed the Dimensions model are strongly biased toward emphasizing Dimension 4, the meaningful use of knowledge. As mentioned previously, according to NAEP's twenty-year summary of performance in reading, writing, mathematics, science, U.S. history, and civics, American students score well on tests that ask them to recall factual information and perform basic content area skills and processes; that is, they perform adequately in Dimension 2, acquiring and integrating procedural knowledge (Mullis et al. 1990). But American students do not perform well on tests that ask them to extend and refine knowledge (Dimension 3) or use knowledge meaningfully (Dimension 4). If assessment drives learning, then learning in Dimensions 3 and 4 can only be improved if assessments emphasize these dimensions. Fortunately, the "authentic assessment" movement advocates exactly this kind of assessment.

Authentic Assessment

The need for authentic assessment is being championed by Wiggins (1989) and many others (Archbald and Newmann 1988, Frederiksen and Collins 1989, Shepard 1989). Wiggins says that if our interest is in evaluating students' abilities to think critically, write graceful prose, and solve real scientific or historical problems, then our tests should ask students to explore literature, write thoughtful and readable prose, and do laboratory or primary-source research. He proposes that such efforts be standard in large-scale assessment. As evidence that such a proposal is feasible, Wiggins cites Great Britain's plan to assess all students between ages seven and sixteen using a variety of tasks that more overtly require the display of such competence. And he asserts that the current rethinking underway in assessment design is best described as a shift to more authentic assessment tasks.

It is no coincidence that the examples of authentic tasks alluded to by Wiggins strongly resemble the types of meaningful-use tasks described in the chapter on Dimension 4. The meaningful-use tasks in Dimension 4 are for the most part "authentic" tasks. That is, decision making, investigation, experimental inquiry, problem solving, and invention are tasks people usually pursue in their day-to-day living. And the meaningful-use tasks of Dimension 4 commonly incorporate many of the extending and refining mental operations described in Dimension 3. As a learner works through an experimental inquiry task, she quite naturally induces and deduces. As she works through a decision-making task, she quite naturally compares and classifies, and so on. This implies that the meaningful-use tasks should drive assessment in any unit of instruction. Although all the dimensions can be assessed, the meaningful-use tasks should receive the most attention.

One way of acting on this principle is to use an assessment profile like that in Figure 7.5 on pages 174 and 175, which Ms. Conklin has decided to use. Note that she has weighted the specific aspects of experimental inquiry that she wants to emphasize. She has also weighted specific aspects of the other four dimensions. Presumably, Ms. Conklin would assign these weights prior to starting the unit and communicate her emphasis to students so that they might know what she considers important. At the end of the unit, Ms. Conklin would then assess each student on the aspects of the five dimensions that she had selected. This figure is a completed evaluation form, showing the evaluation points, how those points are weighted (1 = not very important, 2 = important, 3 = very important), and the final score for each aspect of the dimensions (i.e., evaluation points multiplied by weight).

One of the most powerful features of an assessment profile is that it allows teachers to better quantify student performance. The issue of quantifying performance—assigning scores and grades—is a hotly contested one.

Scores and Grades

Some theorists believe that quantification and grading are incompatible with authentic assessment, particularly where portfolios are concerned. For example, Tierney, Carter, and Desai (1991) say, "We would prefer that portfolios were not scored or graded, but that students' efforts be evaluated through descriptions that illustrate individual strengths and weaknesses" (p. 147). The developers of the Dimensions of Learning model would tend to agree.

Most educators realize, however, that the public's demand to see scores and grades will not soon diminish. In the interim, before qualitative assessment is widely accepted, the best alternative is to spread scores and grades across multiple aspects of performance. In fact, Tierney, Carter, and Desai acknowledge this need: "If they [portfolios] are graded, we would like to see multiple grades differentiating a variety of aspects of student achievement, effort and goals" (p. 147). The assessment profile in Figure 7.5 provides for such varied emphases. For example, Ms. Conklin has decided to assess four of the five dimensions, concentrating on Dimension 4. In the Dimensions of Learning model, quantification does not have to be synonymous with focusing on lower-order knowledge and skills. Multiple aspects of student learning can be incorporated into a score, thus sending a powerful message to students while attending to the public's need for scores and grades.

FIGURE 7.5
An Assessment Profile

	Evaluation 1 2 3 4	Weight 1/3/5	Score
1. Establishing and Maintaining Positive Attitudes and Perceptions			
How well did the student demonstrate positive attitudes and perceptions about:			
• Classroom climate?	3	1	3
• Classroom tasks?	1	1	1
2. Acquiring and Integrating Knowledge			
Student's level of success in understanding and recalling important declarative knowledge	2	5	10
Student's level of success in performing important skills and processes	2	3	6
3. Extending and Refining Knowledge			
Student's level of success in performing specified extending and refining processes and applying them to content knowledge:			
Extending and refining process: __Comparison__			
• Completeness of student's use of the process	4	1	4
• Accuracy and effectiveness of student's thinking during the process	3	3	9
Extending and refining process: __abstracting__			
• Completeness of student's use of the process	1	1	1
• Accuracy and effectiveness of student's thinking during the process	4	3	12

(continued)

FIGURE 7.5
An Assessment Profile
(continued)

	Evaluation				Weight 1/3/5	Score
	1	2	3	4		
4. Meaningful-Use Task						
Completeness of student's use of strategy of experimental inquiry:						
Did the student provide a description of what he or she observed?			3		1	3
Did the student provide an explanation of what he or she observed?		2			1	2
Did the student make a clear prediction?			3		1	3
Did the student plan and carry out an experiment or activity to test the prediction?			3		1	3
Did the student reevaluate the original explanation and change it, if necessary, in light of the outcomes of the experiment or activity?	1				1	1
Accuracy and effectiveness of student's thinking during the experimental inquiry task:						
Was the phenomenon selected by the student for study important?		2			3	6
Was the student's description of the phenomenon comprehensive and complete?			3		3	9
Was the student's explanation of the phenomenon appropriate and accurate?		2			5	10
To what extent did the prediction made by the student logically follow from the student's explanation?		2			5	10
To what extent did the experiment truly test the prediction?			3		5	15
To what extent did the explanation of the outcome of the experiment adequately relate to the student's initial explanation?			3		5	15
5. Habits of Mind						
Did the student demonstrate the habits of mind for:						
• Critical thinking?						
• Creative thinking?			3		1	3
• Self-regulated thinking?		2			3	6

Writing, Speaking, and Symbolizing Across the Curriculum

Although not explicit in the Dimensions model, communication is central to using the dimensions in the classroom. In fact, the Dimensions model incorporates three major movements in education, each of which deals with a specific type of communication. One of the most powerful movements emphasizes "writing across the curriculum"—that is, in all subject areas (Martin 1987, Young and Fulwiler 1986). "Speaking across the curriculum," or developing oral communication skills across the curriculum, is supported by a powerful research base. Cazden (1986) has pointed out that much of the research in this area confirms that oral language is not only the primary method of communicating information in the classroom, but also a primary factor in establishing the climate in which instruction occurs. Still, the level of commitment from educators lags behind that for writing across the curriculum. Perhaps the least well-known communication movement in education, however, is that aimed at increasing the use of symbolism across the curriculum. This effort comes primarily from the field of mathematics. Specifically, the Mathematical Science Education Board (1990) explains that the use of symbolic thinking should be a major goal of mathematics education.

Because writing, speaking, and symbolizing are types of communication, they are all influenced by audience. In general, audience can be thought of as a continuum that runs from *self* to *colleagues* to the *general public*. When the audience for the communication is self, the writing, speaking, or symbolizing is subjective and idiosyncratic. A student can use or not use any convention he wishes, since the communication is meant for his eyes only. When the audience is colleagues, the writing, speaking, or symbolizing must be somewhat more formal, though not as formal as communication meant for the general public. It is important to note that the teacher is usually considered a colleague or coworker. Hence, when writing, speaking, or symbolizing is intended for the teacher only, it is legitimate and, in fact, advantageous to relax expectations about meeting conventions. When the audience is the general public, the tone is formal and, consequently, formal conventions should be followed and the product (i.e., the essay, speech, graph, chart, etc.) should go through successive drafts to ensure high quality.

Figure 7.6 lists various types of written, spoken, and symbolic products that might be used in a unit of instruction and the effects of audience on these products. All three types of communication listed in Figure 7.6 are facilitated by the Dimensions model, particularly those in the third column. Specifically, the emphasis in Dimension 4 on

FIGURE 7.6
Types of Written, Spoken, and Symbolic Products

AUDIENCE

less formal   *more formal*

	Self	Others	Public

SPEAKING	1. self-talk
	2. brainstorming
	3. self-questioning
	4. mental rehearsal
	5. self-prompting
		1. conference with
		   teacher and/or
		   peers
		2. brainstorming
		3. sharing ideas
		4. small-group discussion
		5. classroom discussion
		6. role playing
			1. prepared oral present-
			   ation
			2. dramatic presentation
			3. extemporaneous speech
			4. formal speech
			5. simulation
			6. panel discussion
			7. debate
			8. newscast or interview

WRITING	1. free writing
	2. brainstorming
	3. note taking
	4. listing
		1. note taking
		2. group learning log
		3. rough drafts of:
		   a. written reports
		   b. essays
		   c. stories
		   d. letters
		   e. plays
		   f. skits
		   g. outlines
		   h. computer programs
			1. note taking
			2. group learning log
			3. final drafts of:
			   a. written reports
			   b. essays
			   c. stories
			   d. letters
			   e. plays
			   f. skits
			   g. outlines
			   h. computer programs

SYMBOLIZING	1. doodling
	2. sketching
	3. informal graphic
	   organizers
	4. informal charts,
	   maps, tables, etc.
		1. analogies and
		   metaphors
		2. rough drafts of:
		   a. graphic organizers
		   b. charts, graphs,
		     maps, etc.
		   c. pictures
		   d. poems
		   e. songs
		   f. dance
		   g. video
		   h. models (physical or
		     abstract
		   i. equations
		   j. collages
		   k. sculptures
		   l. pantomime
		   m. flow chart
			1. analogies and
			   metaphors
			2. final drafts of:
			   a. graphic organizers
			   b. charts, graphs,
			     maps, etc.
			   c. pictures
			   d. poems
			   e. songs
			   f. dance
			   g. video
			   h. models (physical or
			     abstract
			   i. equations
			   j. collages
			   k. sculptures
			   l. pantomime
			   m. flow chart

Note: **This chart was developed by members of the Dimensions of Learning Consortium: S. Berman, L. Blust, M. Foseid, L. Kellenbenz, D. MacLean, A. Monetta, and F. Robertson.**

creating products to accompany meaningful-use tasks encourages the use of most, if not all, of the items listed in column 3. For example, as a result of a decision-making task, a student might decide to communicate orally via a panel discussion, or he might elect to communicate in written form through a well-crafted outline. Or he might decide to communicate symbolically through a picture or graphic organizer. Finally (and preferably), the student might elect to use a variety of communication modes that cut across all three categories.

The emphasis in Dimension 4 on products also facilitates the use of the items in column 2 of Figure 7.6, since most of these are rough drafts of the items in column 3. And the emphasis in the Dimensions model on group activities and conferencing encourages the use of many of the items in columns 1 and 2. Communication, then, in all three modes—writing, speaking, and symbolizing—for a variety of audiences is an important theme within the Dimensions model.

Cooperative Learning Across the Curriculum

Cooperative learning is another powerful innovation that is implicit in the Dimensions of Learning model. Davidson and Warsham (1992), Slavin (1983), and Johnson, Johnson, Roy, and Holubec (1984) have developed comprehensive descriptions of cooperative learning. Although cooperative learning can be used to enhance all the dimensions, Dimensions 4 calls for its use most strongly. As described in Chapter 5, one of the major decisions in planning for the meaningful use of knowledge is whether students will work in cooperative groups. The meaningful-use tasks (decision making, investigation, experimental inquiry, problem solving, and invention) are probably done more efficiently by a cooperative group than by an individual, simply because the tasks are so taxing in terms of the knowledge and ability they require to be effectively completed. For instance, all require gathering a lot of information, and a cooperative group can naturally gather more information than an individual. Additionally, a long project can easily exhaust the energy and resources of one person, whereas the energy and resources of a cooperative group will rarely be insufficient to complete lengthy tasks. In short, the very nature of meaningful-use tasks calls for the knowledge, ability, resources, and energy available in cooperative groups.

When meaningful-use tasks are performed in cooperative groups, they promote two important aspects of cooperative learning, group reward and task specialization. Group reward means that the reward for each member of a group depends on all members' learning and performance in completing the task (Slavin 1983). Slavin notes that group rewards based on every group member's performance increase instructional effectiveness because such rewards are likely to motivate students to do whatever is necessary to make it possible for the group to succeed, because no individual can succeed unless the group succeeds.

Slavin also describes the importance of task specialization. Task specialization inherently enhances the quality of the meaningful-use tasks because it maximizes the knowledge, ability, resources, and energy available for each component of the task. Where one student might not have the knowledge necessary to complete a component of an experimental inquiry task, another would; where one student might not have the ability to set up an experiment within such a task, another would. Slavin (1983) notes that for task specialization to be effective, each member of the group must have a specific part of the task to do, group members must depend on one another, and members should not be able to easily substitute for one another in completing the task.

Dimensions of Learning as a Tool for Restructuring

This book began with a call from the U.S. Deputy Secretary of Education to get to the "heart of the matter" of educational reform. The Dimensions of Learning model is meant as a tool—arguably the most powerful tool—for bringing about substantive change in schools. When used in earnest by teachers, administrators, and curriculum developers, it produces compelling results.

Teachers who use the Dimensions model help students direct their own learning by including at least two distinct types of instruction in their classes—one that is more teacher-directed and one that is more student-directed. In doing so, they use a wide variety of teaching strategies that give students varied learning experiences. And they assess their students in ways that are more authentic than those currently used in most schools. Planning under the Dimensions framework is both systematic and creative, extending far beyond a simple review of the next chapter in the textbook.

Administrators who use the Dimensions model find that they must look at a much broader context for supervision. A single lesson is no longer an accurate representation of what occurs in the classroom. Given the diversity of activities in a unit designed according to the Dimensions model, accurate supervision necessarily includes a sampling of presentation and workshop classes at the beginning, middle, and end of a unit. Moreover, the emphasis in the Dimensions model on five distinct types of thinking forces administrators to focus on student behavior rather than teacher behavior as the ultimate source of information regarding the effectiveness of what is happening in the classroom; that is, administrators must look primarily to students for evidence of the five types of thinking and secondarily to teachers for behaviors that elicit the five types of thinking.

Curriculum developers who use the Dimensions model must take a much broader view of the ultimate goals of schooling. Explicit in the model is an emphasis not only on content but also on the attitudes, perceptions, and mental habits necessary to be a self-directed learner. Curriculum design, then, from the Dimensions perspective, must include not only a robust notion of content but a holistic view of the learner.

Learning is a complex process that we may never fully understand. But the work of cognitive researchers has certainly given us a far better understanding than we had twenty or thirty years ago. The problem is that this understanding rarely crosses over to what happens in most American classrooms. Although there has been piecemeal change, our education system is still based on outmoded ideas about learning; as a result, it ultimately fails to prepare many students for the modern world they will live in—a world that will arguably require a lifetime of learning. It's not too late for change, though. By systematically finding out about the dimensions of learning and applying what we learn, we can transform schools into true centers of learning in which students develop the kinds of thinking that will enable them to lead rich and productive lives.

References

Adams, J. E. (1986). *The Biblical View of Self-Esteem, Self-Love, Self-Image.* Eugene, Oreg.: Harvest House Publishers.

Amabile, T. M. (1983). *The Social Psychology of Creativity.* New York: Springer-Verlag.

AAAS. (1989). *Project 2061: Science for All Americans.* Washington, D.C.: American Association for the Advancement of Science.

Anderson, J. (1982). "Acquisition of Cognitive Skills." *Psychological Review* 89: 369–406.

Anderson, J. (1983). *The Architecture of Cognition.* Cambridge, Mass.: Harvard University Press.

Anderson, J. (1990). *Cognitive Psychology and Its Implications.* New York: W. H. Freeman and Company.

Anderson, L., C. Evertson, and E. Emmer. (1980). "Dimensions in Classroom Management Derived from Recent Research." *Journal of Curriculum Studies* 12: 343–356.

Archbald, D. A., and F. M. Newmann. (1988). *Beyond Standardized Testing: Assessing Authentic Achievement in the Secondary School.* Reston, Va.: National Association of Secondary School Principals.

Atwell, N. C. (1987). *In the Middle.* Portsmouth, N.H.: Heinemann.

Ausubel, D. P. (1968) *Educational Psychology: A Cognitive View.* New York: Holt, Rinehart and Winston.

Banathy, B. (1980). "The School: An Autonomous or Cooperating Social Agency." In *Critical Issues in Educational Policy,* edited by L. Rubin. Boston: Allyn and Bacon.

Bartlett, F. C. (1932). *Remembering: A Study in Experimental and Social Psychology.* New York and London: Cambridge University Press.

Beyer, B. K. (1988). *Developing a Thinking Skills Program.* Boston, Mass.: Allyn and Bacon.

Bloom, A. (1987). *The Closing of the American Mind.* New York: Simon and Schuster.

Bloome, D. (1991). "Anthropology and Research in Teaching the English Language Arts." In *Handbook of Research on Teaching the English Language Arts,* edited by J. Flood, J. M. Jensen, D. Lapp, and J. R. Squire. New York: Macmillan.

Bormouth, J. (1968). "The Cloze Readability Procedure." *Elementary English,* 45: 429–436.

Brandt, R. S., ed. (1988). *Content of the Curriculum.* Alexandria, Va.: Association for Supervision and Curriculum Development.

Bransford, J. D., and M. K. Johnson. (1972). "Contextual Prerequisites for Understanding: Some Investigations of Comprehension and Recall." *Journal of Verbal Learning and Verbal Behavior* 11: 717–726.

Bransford, J. D., and B. S. Stein. (1984). *The IDEAL Problem Solver.* New York: Freeman.

Brewer, W. F., and J. C. Treyens. (1981). "Role of Schemata in Memory for Places." *Cognitive Psychology* 13: 207—230.

Britton, J., T. Burgess, N. Martin, A. McLeod, and H. Rosen. (1975). *The Development of Writing Abilities.* London: Macmillan.

Brophy, J. (1982). *Classroom Organization and Management.* Washington, D.C.: National Institute of Education.

Brown, A. L. (1978). "Knowing When, Where and How to Remember: A Problem of Metacognition." In *Advances in Instructional Psychology, Vol. 1,* edited by R. Glaser. Hillsdale, N.J.: Lawrence Erlbaum.

Brown, A. L. (1980). "Metacognitive Development and Reading." In *Theoretical Issues in Reading Comprehension,* edited by R. J. Spiro, B. C. Bruce, and W. F. Brewer. Hillsdale, N.J.: Lawrence Erlbaum.

Brown, J. S., and R. R. Burton. (1978). "Diagnostic Models for Procedural Bugs in Basic Mathematical Skills." *Cognitive Science* 2: 155–192.

Bruner, J. S., J. Goodnow, and G. A. Austin. (1956). *A Study of Thinking*. New York: Wiley.

Burton, R. R. (1982). "Diagnosing Bugs in a Simple Procedural Skill." In *Intelligent Tutoring Systems*, edited by D. Sleeman and J. S. Brown. New York: Academic Press.

California State Board of Education. (1990). *Science Framework for the California Public Schools, Kindergarten Through Grade Twelve.* Sacramento, Calif.: California State Board of Education.

California State Department of Education. (1989). *A Question of Thinking: A First Look at Students' Performance on Open-ended Questions in Mathematics.* Sacramento, Calif.: California State Board of Education.

Calkins, L. M. (1986). *The Art of Teaching Writing.* Portsmouth, N.H.: Heinemann.

Carbo, M., R. Dunn, and K. Dunn. (1986). *Teaching Students to Read Through Their Individual Learning Styles.* Englewood Cliffs, N.J.: Prentice-Hall.

Carey, N., and R. Shavelson. (1989). "Outcomes, Achievement, Participation, and Attitudes." In *Indicators for Monitoring Mathematics and Science Education*, edited by R. J. Shavelson, L. M. McDonnell, and J. Oakes. Santa Monica: RAND Corporation.

Carkhuff, R. R. (1987). *The Art of Helping*, 6th ed. Amherst, Mass.: Human Resource Development Press.

Cazden, C. B. (1986). "Classroom Discourse." In *Handbook of Research on Teaching*, 3rd ed., edited by M. C. Wittrock. New York: Macmillan.

Christenbury, L., and P. P. Kelly. (1983). *Questioning: A Path to Critical Thinking.* Urbana, Ill.: Clearinghouse on Reading and Communication Skills, the National Council of Teachers of English.

Clarke, J. H. (1991). "Using Visual Organizers to Focus on Thinking." *Journal of Readers* 34, 7: 526–534.

Clement, J., J. Lockhead, and G. Mink. (1979). "Translation Difficulties in Learning Mathematics." *American Mathematical Monthly* 88: 3–7.

Combs, A. W. (1962). "A Perceptual View of the Adequate Personality." In *Perceiving, Behaving, Becoming: A New Focus for Education,* edited by A. W.

Combs. Alexandria, Va.: Association for Supervision and Curriculum Development.

Combs, A. W. (1982). *A Personal Approach to Teaching: Beliefs That Make a Difference.* Boston: Allyn & Bacon.

Cooper, C. R. (1983). "Procedures for Describing Written Texts." In *Research on Writing*, edited by P. Mosenthal, L. Tamor, and S. A. Walmsley. New York: Longman.

Cooper, M. M. (1984). "The Pragmatics of Form: How Do Writers Discover What to Do When?" In *New Directions in Composition Research*, edited by R. Beach and L. S. Bridwell. New York: The Guilford Press.

Copi, I. M. (1972). *Introduction to Logic.* New York: Macmillan.

Corey, S. R. (1990). *The Seven Habits of Highly Effective People.* New York: Simon and Schuster.

Costa, A. (19891). "Toward a Model of Human Intellectual Functioning." In *Developing Minds: A Resource Book for Teaching Thinking*, revised edition, edited by A. Costa. Alexandria, Va.: Association for Supervision and Curriculum Development.

Costa, A. L., and R. J. Marzano. (1991). "Teaching the Language of Thinking." In *Developing Minds: A Resource Book for Teaching Thinking,* revised edition, edited by A. Costa. Alexandria, Va.: Association for Supervision and Curriculum Development.

Covington, M. V. (1983). "Motivation Cognitions." In *Learning and Motivation in the Classroom*, edited by S. G. Paris, G. M. Olson and H. W. Stevenson. Hillsdale, N.J.: Lawrence Erlbaum.

Covington, M. V. (1985). "Strategic Thinking and the Fear of Failure." In *Thinking and Learning Skills: Vol. 1, Relating Instruction to Research*, edited by J. W. Segal, S. F. Chipman, and R. Glaser. Hillsdale, N.J.: Lawrence Erlbaum.

Davidson, N., and T. Worsham. (1992). *Enhancing Thinking Through Cooperative Learning.* New York: Teachers College Press.

Davis, R. B. (1984). *Learning Mathematics: The Cognitive Science Approach to Mathematics Education.* Norwood, N.J.: Ablex.

de Bono, E. (1985)."The CoRT Thinking Program." In *Thinking and Learning Skills: Vol. 1, Relating Instruction to Research*, edited by J. W. Segal, S. F. Chipman, and R. Glaser. Hillsdale, N.J.: Lawrence Erlbaum.

Doyle, W. (1983). "Academic Work." *Review of Educational Research* 53: 159–199.

Duncker, K. (1945). "On Problem-Solving." Translated by L. S. Lees. *Psychological Monographs* 58: 270.

Durst, R. K., and G. E. Newell. (1989). "The Uses of Function: James Britton's Category System and Research on Writing." *Review of Educational Research* 59, 4: 375–394.

Ebbinghaus, H. (1897). "Ueber Eine Neue Methode Zur Prufung Geistiger Fahigkeiten und Ihre Anwendung Bei Schulkindern." *Zeitsch Fur Psychologie und Physiologie der Sinnesorgane* 13: 401–457.

Edmonds, R. R. (1982). "Programs of School Improvement: An Overview." *Educational Leadership* 40, 3: 4–11.

Ehrenberg, S. D., L. M. Ehrenberg, and D. Durfee. (1979). *BASICS: Teaching / Learning Strategies*. Miami Beach, Fla.: Institute for Curriculum and Instruction.

Emmer, E. T., C. M. Evertson, and L. Anderson. (1980). "Effective Management at the Beginning of the School Year." *Elementary School Journal* 80: 219–231.

Ennis, R. H. (1985). "Goals for a Critical Thinking Curriculum." In *Developing Minds: A Resource Book for Teaching Thinking*, edited by A. Costa. Alexandria, Va.: Association for Supervision and Curriculum Development.

Ennis, R. H. (1987). "A Taxonomy of Critical Thinking Dispositions and Abilities." In *Teaching Thinking Skills: Theory and Practice*, edited by J. Baron and R. Sternberg. New York: Freeman.

Ennis, R. H. (1989). "Critical Thinking and Subject Specificity: Clarification and Needed Research." *Educational Researcher* 18, 3: 4–10.

Fairbrother, R. (1975). "The Reliability of Teachers' Judgments of the Abilities Being Tested by Multiple Choice Items." *Educational Researcher* 17: 202–210.

Farrell, E. (1991). "Instructional Models for English Language Arts, K–12." In *Handbook of Research on Teaching the English Language Arts*, edited by J. Flood, J. M. Jensen, D. Lapp, and J. R. Squire. New York: Macmillan.

Feuerstein, R., Y. Rand, M. B. Hoffman, and R. Miller. (1980). *Instrumental Enrichment*, Baltimore, Md.: University Park Press.

Fisher, C. W., and D. Berliner, eds. (1985). *Perspectives on Instructional Time*. New York: Longman.

Fisher, C. W., and E. F. Hiebert. (1988). *Characteristics of Literacy Learning Activities in Elementary Schools*. Paper presented at the annual meeting of the National Reading Conference, Tucson, Ariz.

Fisher, R., and W. Ury. (1981). *Getting to Yes*. New York: Penguin Books.

Fitts, P. M., and M. I. Posner. (1967). *Human Performance*. Belmont, Calif.: Brooks Cole.

Flavell, J. H. (1976a). "Metacognitive Aspects of Problem Solving." In *The Nature of Intelligence*, edited by L. B. Resnick. Hillsdale, N.J.: Lawrence Erlbaum.

Flavell, J. H. (1976b). "Metacognition and Cognitive Monitoring: A New Area of Psychological Inquiry." *American Psychologist* 34, 906–911.

Flavell, J. H. (1977). *Cognitive Development*. Englewood Cliffs, N.J.: Prentice-Hall.

Frederiksen, C. H. (1977). "Semantic Processing Units in Understanding Text." In *Discourse Production and Comprehension, Vol 1*, edited by R. O. Freedle. Norwood, N.J.: Ablex.

Frederiksen, J. R., and A. Collins. (1989). "A Systems Approach to Educational Testing." *Educational Researcher* 18, 9: 2–32.

Frederiksen, N. (1984)."Implications of Cognitive Theory for Instruction in Problem Solving." *Review of Educational Research* 54: 363–407.

Fulwiler, T. (1986). "The Argument for Writing Across the Curriculum." In *Writing Across the Disciplines: Research into Practice*, edited by A. Young and T. Fulwiler. Portsmouth, N.H.: Boynton/Cook.

Gagnon, P., and the Bradley Commission on History in the Schools (1989).

Historical Literacy: The Case for History in American Education. Boston: Houghton-Mifflin.

Gardner, H. (1989). "Being Specialized and Comprehensive Knowledge. The Growing Educational Challenge." In *Schooling for Tomorrow*, edited by T. J. Sergiovanni and J. H. Moore. Boston: Allyn & Bacon.

Gardner, M. (1978). *Aha! Insight.* New York: W. H. Freeman and Co.

Gardner, M. (1982). *Aha! Gotcha!* New York: W. H. Freeman and Co.

Gick, M. L., and K. J. Holyoak. (1980). "Analogical Problem Solving." *Cognitive Psychology* 12: 306–355.

Gick, M. L., and K. J. Holyoak. (1983). "Schema Induction and Analogical Transfer." *Cognitive Psychology* 6: 270–292.

Gilovich, T. (1991). *How We Know What Isn't So.* New York: Free Press.

Glaser, R. (1984). "Education and Thinking: The Role of Knowledge." *American Psychologist* 39: 93–104.

Glaser, R. (1985) "Learning and Instructions: A Letter for a Time Capsule." In *Thinking and Learning Skills, Vol. 2*, edited by S. F. Chipman, J. W. Segal, and R. Glaser. Hillsdale, N.J.: Lawrence Erlbaum.

Glasser, W. (1965). *Reality Therapy.* New York: Harper and Row.

Glasser, W. (1969). *Schools Without Failure.* New York: Harper and Row.

Glasser, W. (1981). *Stations of the Mind.* New York: Harper and Row.

Goldman, J. L., G. F. Berquist, and W. E. Coleman. (1989). *The Rhetoric of Western Thought.* Dubuque, Iowa: Kendall/Hunt.

Good, T. L. (1982). "How Teachers' Expectations Affect Results." *American Education* 18, 10: 25–32.

Good, T. L., and J. E. Brophy. (1972). "Behavioral Expression of Teacher Attitudes." *Journal of Educational Psychology* 63, 6: 616–624.

Goodlad, J. I. (1984). *A Place Called School.* New York: McGraw-Hill.

Goodman, K. S., Y. M. Goodman, and W. J. Hood. (1989). *The Whole Language Evaluation Book.* Portsmouth, N.H.: Heinemann.

Gourley, T. J. (1981). "Adapting the Varsity Sports Model to Nonpsychomotor Gifted Students." *Gifted Child Quarterly* 25: 164–166.

Gourley, T. J., and C. S. Micklus. (1982). *Problems, Problems, Problems. Discussion and Activities Designed to Enhance Creativity.* Glassboro, N.J.: Creative Publications.

Halpern, D. F. (1984). *Thought and Knowledge: An Introduction to Critical Thinking.* Hillsdale, N.J.: Lawrence Erlbaum.

Hansen, J. (1987). *When Writers Read.* Portsmouth, N.H.: Heinemann.

Harp, B., ed. (1991). *Assessment and Evaluation in Whole Language Programs.* Norwood, Mass.: Christopher-Gordon Publishers.

Harter, S. (1980). "The Perceived Competence Scale for Children." *Child Development* 51: 218–235.

Harter, S. (1982). "A Developmental Perspective on Some Parameters of Self-Regulation in Children." In *Self-Management and Behavior Change: From Theory to Practice*, edited by P. Karoly and F. H. Kanfer. New York: Pergamon Press.

Hawking, S. (1988). *A Brief History of Time.* New York: Bantam.

Hayes, J. R. (1981). *The Complete Problem Solver.* Philadelphia: The Franklin Institute.

Healy, J. M.(1990). *Endangered Minds: Why Our Children Don't Think.* New York: Simon & Schuster.

Heimlich, J. E., and S. D. Pittelman. (1988). *Semantic Mapping: Classroom Applications.* Newark, Del.: International Reading Association.

Hiebert, J., ed. (1986). *Conceptual and Procedural Knowledge: The Case of Mathematics.* Hillsdale, N.J.: Lawrence Erlbaum.

Hirsch, E. D., Jr. (1987). *Cultural Literacy: What Every American Needs to Know.* Boston: Houghton Mifflin.

Hom, H. L., Jr., and M. D. Murphy. (1983). "Low Need Achiever's Performance: The Positive Impact of a Self-Determined Goal." *Personality and Social Psychology Bulletin* 11: 275–285.

Hunter, M. (1984). "Knowing, Teaching, and Supervising." In *Using What We Know About Teaching*, edited by P. Hosford. Alexandria, Va.: Association for Supervision and Curriculum Development.

Hunter, M. (1969). *Teach More Faster!* El Segundo, Calif.: TIP Publications.

Hunter, M. (1976). *Rx: Improved Instruction.* El Sequndo, Calif.: TIP Publications.

Hunter, M. (1982). *Mastery Teaching.* El Segundo, Calif.: TIP Publications.

Jaques, E. (1985). "Development of Intellectual Capability." In *Essays on the Intellect*, edited by F. R. Link. Alexandria, Va.: Association for Supervision and Curriculum Development.

Johnson, D. W., R. T. Johnson, P. Roy, E. J. Holubec. (1984). *Circles of Learning: Cooperation in the Classroom.* Alexandria, Va.: Association for Supervision and Curriculum Development.

Johnson, D. W., G. Maruyama, R. T. Johnson, D. Nelson, and L. Skon. (1981). "Effects of Cooperative, Competitive and Individual Goal Structure on Achievement: A Meta-analysis." *Psychological Bulletin* 89: 47–62.

Johnson-Laird, P. N. (1975). "Models of Deduction." In *Reasoning: Representation and Process in Children and Adults*, edited by R. J. Falmagne. Hillsdale, N.J.: Lawrence Erlbaum.

Johnson-Laird, P. N. (1983). *Mental Models.* Cambridge, Mass.: Harvard University Press.

Johnson-Laird, P. N. (1985). "Logical Thinking: Does it Occur in Daily Life?" In *Thinking and Learning Skills, Vol. 2: Research and Open Questions*, edited by S. F. Chipman, J. W. Segal and R. Glaser. Hillsdale, N.J.: Lawrence Erlbaum.

Jones, B. F., M. Amiran, and M. Katims. (1985). "Teaching Cognitive Strategies and Text Structures Within Language Arts Programs." In *Thinking and Learning Skills, Vol. 1: Relating Instruction to Research*, edited by J. W. Segal, S. F. Chipman, and R. Glaser. Hillsdale, N.J.: Lawrence Erlbaum.

Jones, B. F., A. S. Palincsar, D. S. Ogle, and E. G. Carr. (1987). *Strategic Teaching: Cognitive Instruction in the Content Areas.* Alexandria, Va.: Association of Supervision and Curriculum Development.

Joyce, B., and M. Weil. (1986). *Models of Teaching.* Englewood Cliffs, N.J.: Prentice-Hall.

Katz, S. E. (1976). *The Effect of Each of Four Instructional Treatments on the Learning of Principles in Children.* Madison: University of Wisconsin, Wisconsin Research and Development Center for Cognition and Learning.

Kearns, D. T. (April 1988). "An Education Recovery Plan for America." *Phi Delta Kappan*: 565–570.

Kerman, S., T. Kimball, and M. Martin. (1980). *Teacher Expectation and Student Achievement: Coordinator's Manual.* Bloomington, Ind.: Phi Delta Kappa.

Kinneavy, J. L. (1991). "Rhetoric." In *Handbook of Research on Teaching the English Language Arts*, edited by J. Flood, J. M. Jensen, D. Lapp and J. R. Squire. New York: Macmillan.

Kintsch, W. (1974). *The Representation of Meaning in Memory.* Hillsdale, N.J.: Lawrence Erlbaum.

Kintsch, W. (1979). "On Modeling Comprehension." *Educational Psychologist* 14: 3–14.

Kintsch, W., and T. A. van Dijk. (1978). "Toward a Model of Text Comprehension and Production." *Psychological Review* 85: 363–394.

Klausmeier, H. J. (1985). *Educational Psychology.* 5th ed. New York: Harper & Row.

Klausmeier, H. J., and T. Sipple. (1980). *Learning and Teaching Concepts.* New York: Academic Press.

Klenk, V. (1983). *Understanding Symbolic Logic.* Englewood Cliffs, N.J.: Prentice-Hall.

Kolers, P. A. (1976). "Reading a Year Later." *Journal of Experimental Psychology: Human Learning and Memory* 2: 554–565.

Kolers, P. A. (1979). "A Pattern Analyzing Basis of Recognition." In *Levels of Processing in Human Memory*, edited by L. S. Cermak and F. I. M. Craik. Hillsdale, N.J.: Lawrence Erlbaum.

LaBerge, D., and S. J. Samuels. (1974). "Toward a Theory of Automatic Information Processing Reading." *Cognitive Psychology* 6: 293–323.

Larkin, J. (1981). "Enriching Formal Knowledge: A Model for Learning to Solve Textbook Physics Problems." In

Cognitive Skills and Their Acquisition, edited by J. R. Anderson. Hillsdale, N.J.: Lawrence Erlbaum.

Lewis, D., and J. Greene. (1982). *Thinking Better.* New York: Holt, Rinehart and Winston.

Lindsay, P. H., and D. A. Norman. (1977). *Human Information Processing.* New York: Academic Press.

Lindsley, O. R. (1972). "From Skinner to Precision Teaching." In *Let's Try Doing Something Else Kind of Thing*, edited by J. B. Jordan and L. S. Robbins. Arlington, Va.: Council on Exceptional Children.

Lipman, M., A. M. Sharp, and F. S. Oscanyan. (1980). *Philosophy in the Classroom.* Philadelphia: Temple University Press.

Lockwood, A. L., and D. E. Harris. (1985). *Reasoning with Democratic Values: Volume 2.* New York: Teacher College Press.

Macrorie, K. (1984). *Writing to be Read.* Upper Montclair, N.J.: Boynton/Cook.

Mandler, G. (1983). "The Nature of Emotions." In *States of Mind*, edited by J. Miller. New York: Pantheon Books.

Markus, H., and A. Ruvulo. (1990). "Possible Selves. Personalized Representations of Goals." In *Goal Concepts in Psychology*, edited by L. Pervin. Hillsdale, N.J.: Lawrence Erlbaum.

Markus, H., and E. Wurf. (1987). "The Dynamic Self-Concept. A Social Psychological Perspective." *Annual Review of Psychology* 38: 299–337.

Marrs, T. (1990). *New Age Cults and Religions.* Austin, Tex.: Living Truth Publishers.

Martin, N., ed. (1987). *Writing Across the Curriculum.* Upper Montclair, N.J.: Boynton/Cook.

Marzano, R. J. (1991). *Cultivating Thinking in English and the Language Arts.* Urbana, Ill.: National Council of Teachers of English.

Marzano, R. J., R. S. Brandt, C. S. Hughes, B. F. Jones, B. Z. Presseisen, S. C. Rankin, and C. Suhor. (1988). *Dimensions of Thinking: A Framework for Curriculum and Instruction.* Alexandria, Va.: Association for Supervision and Curriculum Development.

Marzano, R. J., and A. L. Costa. (1988). "Question: Do Standardized Tests Measure Cognitive Skills? Answer: No." *Educational Leadership* 45: 66–73.

Marzano, R. J., and D. M. Jesse. (1987). *A Study of General Cognitive Operations in Two Achievement Test Batteries and Their Relationship to Item Difficulty.* (Technical Report). Aurora, Colo.: Mid-continent Regional Educational Laboratory.

Marzano, R. J., D. J. Pickering, D. E. Arredondo, G. J. Blackburn, R. S. Brandt, C. A. Moffett. (1992). *Dimensions of Learning Teacher's Manual.* Alexandria, Va.: Association for Supervision and Curriculum Development.

Maslow, A. H. (1968). *Toward a Psychology of Being.* New York: Van Nostrand Reinhold.

Mathematical Science Education Board (1990). *Reshaping School Mathematics.* Washington D.C.: National Academy Press.

McCarthy, B. (1980). *The 4MAT System.* Oak Harbor, Ill.: Excel, Inc.

McCarthy, B. (1990). "Using the 4MAT System to Bring Learning Styles to Schools." *Educational Leadership* 48, 2: 31–37.

McCombs, B. L. (1984). "Processes and Skills Underlying Intrinsic Motivation to Learn: Toward a Definition of Motivational Skills Training Intervention." *Educational Psychologist* 19: 197–218.

McCombs, B. L. (1986). "The Role of the Self-System in Self-Regulated Learning." *Contemporary Educational Psychology* 11: 314–332.

McCombs, B. L. (April 1987). *Issues in the Measurement by Standardized Tests of Primary Motivation Variables Related to Self-Regulated Learning.* Paper presented at the annual meeting of the American Educational Research Association, Washington, D.C.

McCombs, B. L. (1989). "Self-Regulated Learning and Academic Achievement: A Phenomenological View." In *Self-Regulated Learning and Academic Achievement: Theory Research and Practice*, edited by B. J. Zimmerman and D. H. Schunk. New York: Springer-Verlag.

McCombs, B. L., and R. J. Marzano. (1990). "Putting the Self in Self-Regulated Learning: The Self as Agent in Integrating Will and Skill." *Educational Psychologist* 25, 1: 51–69.

McTighe, J., and F. T. Lyman, Jr. (1988). "Cueing Thinking in the Classroom: The Promise of Theory Embedded Tools." *Educational Leadership* 45, 7: 18–25.

Meichenbaum, D. (1977). *Cognitive Behavior Modification.* New York: Plenum Press.

Mervis, C. B. (1980). "Category Structure and the Development of Categorization." In *Theoretical Issues in Reading Comprehension*, edited by R. J. Sprio, B. C. Bruce and W. F. Brewer. Hillsdale, N.J.: Lawrence Erlbaum.

Meyer, B. J. F. (1975). *The Organization of Prose and Its Effects on Memory.* New York: American Elsevier.

Miller, G. A., E. Galanter, and K. H. Pribram. (1960). *Plans and the Structure of Behavior.* New York: Holt, Rinehart and Winston.

Mills, R. C. (April 1987). *Relationship Between School Motivational Climate, Teacher Attitudes, Student Mental Health, School Failure and Health Damaging Behavior.* A paper presented at the annual conference of the American Educational Research Association, Washington, D.C.

Mills, R. C., R. G. Dunham, and G. P. Alpert. (1988). "Working with High-Risk Youth on Prevention and Early Intervention Programs: Toward a Comprehensive Model." *Adolescence* 23, 91: 643–660.

Morrow, L. M. (1991). "Promoting Voluntary Reading." In *Handbook of Research on Teaching the English Language Arts*, edited by J. Flood, J. M. Jensen, D. Lapp and J. R. Squire. New York: Macmillan.

Mullis, I. V. S., E. H. Owen, and G. W. Phillips (1990). *America's Challenge: Accelerating Academic Achievement (A Summary of Findings from 20 Years of NAEP).* Princeton, N.J.: Educational Testing Service.

Naisbitt, J. (1982). *Megatrends.* New York: Warner Books.

NCTM (1989). *Curriculum and Evaluation Standards for School Mathematics.* Reston, Va.: National Council of Teachers of Mathematics.

Nickerson, R. S., D. N. Perkins, and E. E. Smith. (1985). *The Teaching of Thinking.* Hillsdale, N.J.:Lawrence Erlbaum.

Ogle, D. (1986). "The K-W-L: A Teaching Model that Develops Active Reading of Expository Text." *The Reading Teacher* 39: 564–576.

Ortony, A. (1980). "Metaphor." In *Theoretical Issues in Reading Comprehension*, edited by R. J. Spiro, B. C. Bruce and W. F. Brewer. Hillsdale, N.J.: Lawrence Erlbaum.

Owens, J., G. H. Bower, and J. B. Black. (1979). "The 'Soap Opera' Effect in Story Recall." *Memory and Cognition* 7: 185–191.

Paris, S. G., and B. K. Lindauer. (1982). "The Development of Cognitive Skills During Childhood." In *Handbook of Developmental Psychology*, edited by B. W. Wolman. Englewood Cliffs, N.J.: Prentice-Hall.

Paris, S. G., M. Y. Lipson, and K. K. Wixson. (1983). "Becoming a Strategic Reader." *Contemporary Educational Psychology* 8: 293–316.

Paul, R. (1990). "Socratic Questioning." In *Critical Thinking: What Every Person Needs to Survive in a Rapidly Changing World*, edited by R. Paul. Rohnert Park, Calif.: Sonoma State University, Center for Critical Thinking and Moral Critique.

Paul, R. ed. (1990). *Critical Thinking: What Every Person Needs to Survive in a Rapidly Changing World.* Rohnert Park, Calif.: Center for Critical Thinking and Moral Critique.

Paul, R., A. S. A. Binker, and M. Charbonneau. (1986). *Critical Thinking Handbook: K–3. A Guide for Remodeling Lesson Plans in Language Arts, Social Studies, and Science.* Rohnert Park, Calif.: Sonoma State University, Center for Critical Thinking and Moral Critique.

Paul, R., A. J. A. Binker, D. Martin, C. Vetrano, and H. Kreklau. (1989). *Critical Thinking Handbook: Grades 6–9.* Rohnert Park, Calif.: Center for Critical Thinking and Moral Critique.

Paul, R. W. (1984). "Critical Thinking: Fundamental to Education for a Free

Society." *Educational Leadership* 42, 1: 4–14.

Paul, R. W. (1987). "Critical Thinking and the Critical Person." In *Thinking: Report on Research*. Hillsdale, N.J.: Lawrence Erlbaum.

Perkins, D. N. (1981). *The Mind's Best Work*. Cambridge, Mass.: Harvard University Press.

Perkins, D. N. (1984). "Creativity By Design." *Educational Leadership* 42: 18–25.

Perkins, D. N. (1985). *Where Is Creativity?* Paper presented at University of Iowa Second Annual Humanities Symposium, Iowa City, Iowa.

Perkins, D. N. (1986). *Knowledge as Design*. Hillsdale, N.J.: Lawrence Erlbaum.

Perkins, D. (1989). "Selecting Fertile Themes for Integrated Learning." In *Interdisciplinary Curriculum: Design and Implementation*, edited by H. H. Jacobs. Alexandria, Va.: Association for Supervision and Curriculum Development.

Perkins, D. N., R. Allen, and J. Hafner. (1983). "Difficulties in Everyday Reasoning." In *Thinking: The Expanding Frontier*, edited by W. Maxwell. Philadelphia: The Franklin Institute Press.

Piaget, J. (1954). *The Construction of Reality in the Child*. New York: Basic Books.

Piaget, J. (1959). *Language and Thought of the Child*. Cleveland, Ohio: World.

Piaget, J. (1971). *Genetic Epistemology*, translated by E. Duckworth. New York: Norton.

Pittelman, S. D., J. E. Heimlich, R. L. Berglund, and M. P. French. (1991). *Semantic Feature Analysis: Classroom Applications*. Newark, Del.: International Reading Association.

Pogrow, S. (1991). "HOTS." In *Developing Minds: Programs for Teaching Thinking*, edited by A. Costa. Alexandria, Va.: Association for Supervision and Curriculum Development.

Polya, G. (1957). *How to Solve It*. Princeton, N.J.: University Press.

Powell, A. G., E. Farrar, and D. K. Cohen. (1985). *The Shopping Mall High School*. Boston: Houghton Mifflin.

Powers, W. T. (1973) *Behavior: The Control of Perception*. Chicago: Aldine.

Ravitch, D., and C. E. Finn, Jr. (1987). *What Do Our 17-Year-Olds Know? A Report on the First National Assessment of History and Literature*. New York: Harper and Row.

Resnick, L. B. (1987). *Education and Learning to Think*. Washington, D.C.: National Academy Press.

Romberg, T. A., and T. P. Carpenter. (1986). "Research on Teaching and Learning Mathematics: Two Disciplines of Scientific Inquiry." In *Handbook of Research on Teaching*, 3rd ed., edited by M. C. Wittrock. New York: Macmillan.

Rosenshine, B. (1983)."Teaching Functions in Instructional Programs." *Elementary School Journal* 83, 4: 335–351.

Rosenshine, B. V. (1986). "Synthesis of Research on Explicit Teaching." *Educational Leadership* 43: 60–69.

Ross, J., and K. A. Lawrence. (1968). "Some Observations on Memory Artifice." *Psychonomic Science* 13: 107–108.

Roth, K. J. (1990). "Developing Meaningful Conceptual Understanding in Science." In *Dimensions of Thinking and Cognitive Instruction*, edited by B. J. Jones and L. Idol. Hillsdale, N.J.: Lawrence Erlbaum.

Rowe, H. (1985). *Problem Solving and Intelligence*. Hillsdale, N.J.: Lawrence Erlbaum.

Rumelhart, D. E., and D. A. Norman. (1981). "Accretion, Tuning and Restructuring: Three Modes of Learning." In *Semantic Factors in Cognition*, edited by J. W. Colton and R. Klatzky. Hillsdale, N.J.: Lawrence Erlbaum.

Santostefano, S. (1986). "Cognitive Controls, Metaphors and Contexts. An Approach to Cognition and Emotion." In *Thought and Emotions: Developmental Perspectives*, edited by D. J. Bearson and H. Zimiles. Hillsdale, N.J.: Lawrence Erlbaum.

Sapir, E. (1921). *Language: An Introduction to the Study of Speech*. New York: Harcourt Brace Jovanovich.

Sapir, E. (1961). *Culture, Language and Personality*. Berkeley, Calif.: University of California Press.

❖

Schunk, D. H. (1985). "Participation in Goal Setting: Effects on Self-Efficacy and Skills of Learning Disabled Children." *Journal of Speech Education* 19: 307–317.

Schunk, D. H. (1990)."Goal Setting and Self-Efficacy During Self-Regulated Learning." *Educational Psychologist* 25, 1: 71–86.

Shepard, L. (1989). "Why We Need Better Assessments." *Educational Leadership* 46, 7: 41–47.

Shiffrin, R. M., and W. Schneider. (1977). "Controlled and Automatic Human Information Procesing: II. Perceptual Learning, Automatic Attending, and a General Theory." *Psychological Review* 84: 127–190.

Shipman, V. (1983). *New Jersey Test of Reasoning Skills.* Upper Montclair, N.J.: Montclair State University.

Silver, E. A., and S. P. Marshall. (1990). "Mathematical and Scientific Problem Solving: Findings, Issues, and Instructional Implications." In *Dimensions of Thinking and Cognitive Instruction*, edited by B. J. Jones and L. Idol. Hillsdale, N.J.: Lawrence Erlbaum.

Singly, K., and J. R. Anderson. (1989). *The Transfer of Cognitive Skill.* Cambridge, Mass.: Harvard University Press.

Slavin, R. E. (1983). *Cooperative Learning.* New York: Longman.

Smith, E. E., and D. L. Medin. (1981). *Categories and Concepts.* Cambridge, Mass.,: Harvard University Press.

Smith, F. (1982). *Understanding Reading.* New York: Holt, Rinehart and Winston.

Snowman, J., and R. McCown. (April 1984). *Cognitive Processes in Learning: A Model for Investigating Strategies and Tactics.* Paper presented at the annual meeting of the American Educational Research Association, New Orleans, La.

Spady, W. G. (1988). "Organizing for Results: The Basis of Authentic Restructuring and Reform." *Educational Leadership* 46, 2: 4–8.

Spiro, R. J., W. L. Vispoel, J. G. Schmitz, A. Samarapungauan, and A. E. Boerger. (1987). "Knowledge Acquisition for Application: Cognitive Flexibility and Transfer in Complex Content Domains." In *Executive Control Processes*, edited by B.C. Britton and S.

Glynn. Hillsdale, N.J.: Lawrence Erlbaum.

Stahl, R. J. (1985). "Cognitive Information Processes and Processing Within a Uniprocess and Processing Within a Uniprocess Superstructure/ Microstructure Framework: A Practical Information-Based Model." Unpublished manuscript, University of Arizona, Tucson.

Stauffer, R. (1970). *The Language-Experience Approach to the Teaching of Reading.* New York: Harper and Row.

Swartz, R. J. (1987). *Reading and Thinking: A New Framework for Comprehension.* Boston: Massachusetts Department of Education.

Taba, H. (1967). *Teacher's Handbook for Elementary Social Studies.* Reading, Mass.: Addison-Wesley.

Taylor, W. (1953). "Cloze Procedure: A New Tool for Measuring Readability." *Journalism Quarterly* 30: 415–433.

Thorndike, E. L. (1906). *Principles of Teaching.* New York: A. G. Seiler.

Thorndike, E. L., and R. S. Woodworth. (1901). "The Influence of Improvement in One Mental Function Upon the Efficiency of Other Functions." *Psychological Review* 9: 374–382.

Tierney, R. J., M. A. Carter, and L. F. Desai. (1991). *Portfolio Assessment in the Reading-Writing Classroom.* Norwood, Mass.: Christopher-Gordon Publishers.

Toulmin, S. (1958). *The Uses of Argument.* Cambridge, Mass.: Cambridge University Press.

Toulmin, S., R. Rieke, and A. Janik. (1981). *An Introduction to Reasoning.* New York: Macmillan.

van Dijk, T. A. (1977). *Text and Context.* London: Longman.

van Dijk, T. A. (1980). *Macrostructures.* Hillsdale, N.J.: Lawrence Erlbaum.

van Dijk, T. A., and W. Kintsch. (1983). *Strategies of Discourse Comprehension.* Hillsdale, N.J.: Lawrence Erlbaum.

von Oech, R. (1983). *A Whack on the Side of the Head.* New York: Warner Books.

Vygotsky, L. S. (1978). *Mind in Society: The Development of Higher Psychological Processes*, edited by M. Cole, V. John-Steiner, S. Scritmer, and E. Souberman. Cambridge, Mass.: Harvard University Press.

Vosniadou, S., and W. F. Brewer. (1987). "Theories of Knowledge Restructuring and Development." *Review of Educational Research* 57: 51–67.

Wales, C. E., and A. H. Nardi. (1985). "Teaching Decision-Making: What to Teach and How to Teach It." In *Developing Minds: A Resource Book for Teaching Thinking*, edited by A. L. Costa. Alexandria, Va.: Association for Supervision and Curriculum Development.

Wason, P. C., and P. N. Johnson-Laird. (1972). *Psychology of Reasoning: Structure and Content.* Cambridge, Mass.: Harvard University Press.

Weiner, B. (1972). "Attribution Theory, Achievement Motivation and the Educational Process." *Review of Educational Research* 42: 203–215.

Weiner, B. (1983). "Speculations Regarding the Role of Affect in Achievement-Change Programs Guided by Attributional Principals." In *Teaching and Student Perceptions: Implications for Learning*, edited by J. M. Levine and M. C. Wang. Hillsdale, N.J.: Lawrence Erlbaum.

Whimbey, A., and J. Lockhead. (1985). *Problem Solving and Comprehension.* Hillsdale, N.J.: Lawrence Erlbaum.

Wickelgren, W. A. (1974). *How to Solve Problems.* San Francisco, Calif.: Walt Freeman.

Wickelgren, W. A. (1979). *Cognitive Psychology.* Englewood Cliffs, N.J.: Prentice Hall.

Wiggins, G. (1989). "Teaching to the (Authentic) Test." *Educational Leadership* 46, 7: 41–47.

Williamson, J. (1990). "The Greensboro Plan: A Sample Staff Development Plan." In *Critical Thinking: What Every Person Needs to Survive in a Rapidly Changing World*, edited by R. Paul. Rohnert Park, Calif.: Center for Critical Thinking and Moral Critique, Sonoma State University.

Wood, R. (1977). "Multiple Choice: A State of the Art Report." *Evaluation in Education* 1: 191–280.

Young, A., and T. Fulwiler, eds. (1986). *Writing Across the Disciplines.* Portsmouth, N.H.: Heinemann.

Yussen, S. R., ed. (1985). *The Growth of Reflection in Children.* New York: Academic Press.

About the Author

Robert J. Marzano is Deputy Director of Training and Development, Mid-continent Regional Educational Laboratory, 2550 South Parker Rd., Suite 500, Aurora, Colorado 80014. During his twenty years in education, he has written about such diverse topics as reading and writing instruction, the teaching of thinking, and educational reform.

❖

Current ASCD Networks

❖

ASCD sponsors numerous networks that help members exchange
ideas, share common interests, identify and solve problems, grow
professionally, and establish collegial relationships. The following
networks may be of particular interest to readers of this book:

Authentic Assessment

Contact: Albert Koshiyama, Administrator, School Interventions Unit,
California Dept. of Education, 502 J St., Sacramento, CA 95814-2312.
TEL (916) 324-4933   FAX (916) 327-4239

**Clearinghouse for Learning/Teaching Styles and Brain
Behavior**

Contact: Lois LaShell, Director, Educational Outreach, Antioch
University, 1050 President St., Yellow Springs, OH 45387.
TEL (513) 767-7331, x231   FAX (513) 767-1891

Cooperative Learning

Contact: Harlan Rimmerman, Director, Elementary Education,
Kansas City, Kansas, Schools, 625 Minnesota Ave., Kansas City, KS
66101. TEL (913) 551-3200   FAX (913) 551-3217

Invitational Education

Contact: Dean Fink, Superintendent of Instructional Services, Halton
Board of Education, 2050 Guelph Line, P.O Box 5005, Burlington,
Ontario, CANADA. TEL (416) 335-3663 FAX (416) 335-9802

Learning Community

Contact: F. James Clatworthy, School of Education, Oakland University, Rochester, MI 48309-4401. TEL (313) 370-3052 FAX (313) 370-4202

Network for Restructured Schools

Contact: Florence Seldin, Center for Field Service and Studies, University of Massachusetts–Lowell, One University Ave., Lowell, MA 01854. TEL (508) 934-4601   FAX (508) 934-3005

Student Empowerment for Lifelong Learning

Contact: Diane Cardinalli, 71781 San Gorgonio, Rancho Mirage, CA 92270.   TEL (619) 346-8187

Teaching Thinking

Contact: Robin Fogarty (re: newsletter), Skylight Publishing, Inc., 200 East Wood St., Suite 250, Palatine, IL 60067.   TEL (708) 991-6300 FAX (703) 991-6420; Esther Fusco (re: events), 24 Hopewell Dr., Stony Brook, NY 11790.   TEL (516) 661-5820 FAX (516) 661-4886 (please call first if sending via FAX)

Thinking Assessment

Contact: Sally Duff, Maryland Center for Thinking Studies, Coppin State College, 2500 West North Ave., Baltimore, MD 21216. TEL (301) 396-9362 or 9206